Anne & Alan
Bromberg
1982

A Writer's Capital

A
WRITER'S
CAPITAL

By Louis Auchincloss

*It has been said that his childhood
is a writer's entire capital.*

University of Minnesota Press □ Minneapolis

Printed in the United States of America
at the University of Minnesota Printing Department, Minneapolis.
Published in the United Kingdom and India by the Oxford University
Press, London and Delhi, and in Canada
by the Copp Clark Publishing Co. Limited, Toronto

Library of Congress Catalog Card Number: 73-90568

ISBN 0-8166-0707-9

For Adele and my sons, John, Blake, and Andrew, who came into my life after this memoir ends but who have been responsible for the good things that have happened since.

CONTENTS

PART ONE

How I Became a Writer

BACKGROUND

Snobbery about ancestors varies with the generations. When one of my father's uncles went back to Scotland to look for titles in the family tree, he was only doing what hundreds of his contemporaries had done. Playing golf in Paisley, the ancestral town, he asked his caddie if he had ever heard the name "Auchincloss." The caddie replied that he had. It was his own name. Undeterred by this suggestion of less than Olympian social origin, my great-uncle persisted with his task and came home with an expensive chart, bristling with coats of arms, knighthoods, and royal grants.

Not so inclined was my father's generation. By then the fashion was to have come up from the mud — provided the mud was far enough in the past. A simple origin was deemed indicative of vigor. Father used to boast that the Auchinclosses had been sheep stealers in Ayrshire. But when I went to Paisley I found the tomb of my great-great-grandfather, John Auchincloss, last of our line to die in the old country, in an honorable position at the base of the tower of Paisley Abbey. He had been buried in one grave with his wife and five infant

11

children under a headstone that describes him simply as "Merchant." So the answer was simple. The family had been in Scotland pretty much what they became in New York.

John's son Hugh sailed to Manhattan in 1803, on a ship appropriately called the *Factor*, to establish an American branch of the family dry goods business. When he died, more than fifty years later, he had established both a business and a family. I cannot altogether repress a sigh at the negatives of the Presbyterian parson's funeral oration:

"The fibre of his nature was strong rather than delicate, hence some misapprehended him as harsh and blunt. In our church courts he was known for his sturdy adherence to the more rigid opinions of those who are designated the Old School of Presbyterians. The deceased was not a man of smooth words or disguised flatteries nor even prone to seek good things by craft or indirectness. Making no pretensions to literary culture, he dwelt more in forcible reasons than fair speeches."

One is sure that he did!

I say that he established a family. But is that anything more than a certain proportion of males with the family surname? I have before me a recently compiled genealogical tree of the descendants of Commodore Vanderbilt. Of the 786 of these (of whom my wife is one), only twenty-five were males bearing the surname Vanderbilt. But in 1957, of the 330 descendants of Hugh's son John, fifty-seven were males with the family surname. Add to this that the bulk of these descendants remained in or near New York City and that the name was unique to our family, and you have the beginnings of a clan.

Obviously, with the passage of a very few generations the common denominator of a name is not going to provide more than a superficial link between one man's descendants. In Europe royal and aristocratic families managed to preserve a characteristic appearance by what we regard as almost incestuous marriages. Only two descendants of Hugh intermarried.

12

BACKGROUND

Yet up until World War I some Auchincloss characteristics still lingered. The earlier members of the family stare out of my album with grave, watery eyes over huge aquiline noses. They must have been as dour and plain as their brownstone houses. Even as late as my childhood, my father's maiden aunt, Ellie Auchincloss, expressed disapproval of the sexes using the same swimming pool in Bar Harbor. The later generations changed, of course — the Episcopalian wives brought a lighter, more social note — but some of the flavor of that earlier time persisted in dark, heavy pieces of inherited furniture, in remembered anecdotes of an almost childish simplicity, in our very gratitude that we had escaped the old rigor.

There was never an Auchincloss fortune. Some New York families have a "robber baron" founder, as others have a colonial governor, and Roman ones a pope. But each generation of Auchincloss men either made or married its own money. My father, one of five children with living parents, was able at twenty-five to marry a still unendowed girl, but only by virtue of an allowance from his father of five thousand dollars a year and the loan by his mother-in-law of a floor of her house at 30 West 49th Street. Life was easier then — for some. Seven years later, in 1918, when my mother took me, an infant, and my older brother and sister to Louisville, where Father was in officers' training camp, four Irish maids went with her, and nobody suggested that this was an excessive luxury for a young lawyer's wife.

I was a New Yorker not only through the Auchinclosses. My parents, my grandparents, my eight great-grandparents, all lived in the city. Yet it never seemed to me that there was any dullness of uniformity necessarily inherent in this. Each branch of the tree seemed totally separate from every other. My grandmother Auchincloss's family, for example, the Russells and Howlands, struck me as a different species altogether from the Auchinclosses. They were of English origin and had once held

13

themselves very high, having belonged to the richest class of merchants and bankers before the American Civil War. Their decline had been long, but there was still a faint echo of ancient distinction in the portraits, or copies of portraits, by Peale or Mount, in oft-quoted passages from Mayor Hone's diary about old balls and weddings, in handsomely printed private memorials of the long dead, in a dim nostalgia for days of a simpler Newport, of a gentleman's world of good talk and fine wines. I contrasted all this, at an early age, with the characteristics of the same family in slow, chattering decline: dowdiness in dress and appearance, resentment of new fortunes, cheerful and insincere professions of egalitarianism, Christmas cards with long, fatuous accounts of the petty activities of children and grandchildren. I compared it grimly with the rising Auchinclosses and their smarter women folk.

And then there were the Dixons, my grandmother Stanton's family, a third and totally distinct affair. They really were a clan, or had been, bound together by tight tribal loyalties that had not yet altogether disintegrated in the 1920s. They were handsome, sports-loving, card-playing, smartly dressed, unintellectual, worldly-wise, yet at the same time simple, affectionate, easily homesick, scornful of "lugs," a touch naive, charming. Brooklyn was their origin, but when the oldest sister had made a good match to one of the Sloane brothers, rug merchants, her six siblings had followed her across the East River to Manhattan and settled in brownstones on 49th Street between Fifth and Sixth avenues (it became known as "Dixon Alley"). Even in summer they hated to be separated and occupied a row of shingle cottages on the dunes at Southampton. My mother as a girl had always to check that an aunt did not need a shopping or driving companion before she had an afternoon to herself. On the other hand, parties were made less cruel for a miserably shy debutante by the hovering presence of handsome male cousins who had been told to "keep an eye on

14

Priscilla." One of these, Courtland Dixon, used to tell his friend Howland Auchincloss, at Yale, that he had "just the girl for him." Indeed, he had. It was the flavor of the Dixon family that I tried to catch in *Portrait in Brownstone*, their quickness, their easy laughter, their common sense, their belief of "nothing in excess" — except possibly in family feeling.

When I am told that I have confined my fiction to too small a world, I find it difficult to comprehend. For it seems to me as if I should never come to the end of the variety of types represented by my relatives alone. Auchinclosses, Russells, Dixons, Stantons, how could anyone lump such people into one mold? Was there any common denominator besides humanity itself between that maiden great-aunt who frowned at mixed bathing and my mother's elegant, alcoholic uncle, Edmund Stanton, a mauve decade dandy who sent his shirts abroad to be laundered and who, as director of the Metropolitan, had introduced German opera to New York? Aunt Ellie and Uncle Ed — what an impossible interview!

But these things, I suppose, are measured by the viewing distance. To the untutored eye all horses look alike from the stands. And sometimes even to the tutored. There are moments when I see two cousins of mine, not related to each other, not even aware that they share me as common kin, lunching together at a club, and it suddenly seems to me that they *are* alike, that the divisions in my mind have been imaginary, that there *is* a dull, brownstone New York, as dull as a society reporter's page in an evening paper, and that if one took all those Auchinclosses and Russells and Dixons and Stantons and mixed them up together, one might never get them apart again. And then a particular kind of leaden depression enters my soul. The lights seem to go out. Fortunately, this mood does not last.

Like most children of affluence, I grew up with the distinct sense that my parents were only tolerably well off. This is because children always compare their families with wealthier ones, never with poorer. I thought I knew perfectly what it meant to be rich in New York. If you were rich, you lived in a house with a pompous beaux-arts façade and kept a butler and gave children's parties with spun sugar on the ice cream and little cups of real silver as game prizes. If you were not rich you lived in a brownstone with Irish maids who never called you "Master Louis" and parents who hollered up and down the stairway instead of ringing bells. Father confirmed my sense of our relative poverty by constantly emphasizing that we were ordinary, middle-class Americans. He used even to take us on Sunday afternoon drives in conscious emulation of what he called a great American custom. He and Mother were determined that we should not get any ideas about being "special." What they never entirely took in was that I did not dispute their classification. I was simply ashamed of it. I once suggested to Mother that she go to work like Father. With two earned incomes we might be rich enough to keep a Rolls-Royce!

But one never gets far discussing who is rich and who isn't. One can only state the facts. By 1927, when I was ten, we lived in the winter in a brownstone house on 91st Street with two nurses, a cook, a kitchen maid, a waitress, and a chambermaid. We had a summer house on Long Island which a caretaker later kept open for winter weekends. For July and August we rented a large shingle cottage in Bar Harbor. We had a chauffeur and two cars, which rose to four as the children learned to drive. My parents belonged to half a dozen clubs. And all this was maintained on an annual income of less than a hundred thousand dollars, out of which Father was able to make substantial savings.

When I think of my life in the 1920s and 1930s I am apt to think of crowds. There were all the uncles and aunts and first cousins who assembled at big Christmas parties at my grandparents', and beyond these the dozens of more distant relatives. There were all the boys at school and at my summer sports classes and all the children at the beach clubs of Long Island and Maine. Later, there were the mobs at boarding school and neighboring boarding schools and again at Yale. There were all the girls at the many subscription dances which culminated in the debutante parties, sometimes numbering more than a thousand guests. And then came law school, and finally the war, like an ultimate postgraduate course, with multitudes of one's contemporaries proliferating all over the world. My fellow officers on the LSTs 980 and 130 used to say that I could find a drinking acquaintance in the officers' bar of any atoll or harbor that we happened to visit. I would have had a defective memory had it not been so.

I think the point is worth mentioning, if only because the same critics who complain of the limited scope of my fiction are apt to refer to the New York social world in which I grew up as "small." It was small, like all worlds, in the sense that it was not representative of the population of the United States. And it may indeed, also like other worlds, have been small in spirit. But not only was it not small numerically, it was open-ended. One could, if one wanted, meet almost anybody in it. Its many prejudices were not binding, as they might have been in a small town, on individuals. This may have been simply because in a large city they were unenforceable. Of course, there were stale little pockets of "old New York" where people smirked at the mere sound of a new name, but one did not have to stay in these. My parents were inclined to be lazy about entertaining, but they loved people and were popular, and through such friends as John W. Davis, Judge Learned Hand, Arthur Train, and the family of Walter Damrosch, doors were opened for them into the worlds of politics, arts, and letters. I do not mean to imply that they had a "salon," but simply that they could have, had they cared enough.

That, I submit, was always the thing about New York. One could do anything if one cared enough. Perhaps that is why I have always regarded it as so particularly ignominious for a New Yorker of my generation and upbringing to have failed to enjoy life. There were so many opportunities to do so. Now I realize that this sounds fatuous. We know that opportunities are illusory if the human being is disqualified, by defects of character, to grasp them. That was almost my fate, as this memoir will show. What I am saying is that the opportunities were always there.

MY PARENTS

My FATHER spent his whole professional life of fifty-seven years in a single law firm. He joined Stetson, Jennings & Russell (Russell was his uncle) in 1911 and became a partner ten years later. Thereafter the firm was reorganized by John W. Davis, who had run for the presidency against Calvin Coolidge, and it has since been known by different names, but always familiarly under the abbreviation "Davis Polk." Father's uncle was a bit of a front man, an elegant if rather pompous old-city type, but Father himself was a worker. He specialized in corporate trust indentures, not a career of which the law student is apt to dream, and he was widely respected for his detailed and accurate work. I remember his telling me that a Japanese client had once accused him of leaving an important fact out of a bond indenture. "What?" Father demanded. "The fact that the sun will rise tomorrow."

But Father's great love was more of his firm than his work. He enjoyed his work, but this enjoyment never approached the intense pleasure that he derived from his association with his partners and with the younger men. Davis Polk was not only his office; it was his fraternity, his club, almost, in a way, his church. In his old age, semiretired, he used to lunch daily at the partners' table at his lunch club in order to keep up with the firm news. He was always popular with men. As a youth he had been handsome and athletic, and he had enjoyed the rather noisy camaraderie of the boola, boola Yale of 1908. But nothing meant more to him than the concept of friendship united with professional association. He trusted and loved his partners, and his feelings were returned. I believe that he used intentionally to idealize his firm when he described it to me. It took me years to discover that there never could have been a firm quite like *his* Davis Polk.

Outside the office Father's interests were principally in his home. He liked golf and tennis; he liked to play the piano and the violin; but these things fitted easily into family life. None of his three sons inherited his aptitude for sports, nor were they popular in school or college in the way he had been. If he was disappointed — and I believe he was — he never showed it by so much as a wink. Whatever we were interested in — well, that was the thing about which he would exclaim. Mother would protest loudly when she found me on a beautiful summer afternoon hiding away in the darkest corner of the library reading *The Martyrdom of an Empress* or some similar trash. Not Father. He would try, charmingly if unsuccessfully, to build a bridge between my book and the tennis court. I laughed at his arguments, but I loved him for trying, for caring. The generosity with which he always put his wife and children first touched me at an age when children are not usually touched. He was a genuinely humble man.

Perhaps too much so. There was a sadness in Father, never articulated, indeed constantly repudiated by his own self-mockery. We knew that he had been taken out of Groton as a sixth former for several months — inexplicably. The same thing had happened, for a much shorter time, in law school. In his fifties he was to suffer a couple of bad nervous breakdowns which would put serious kinks in his legal career. But that was later. When we were young, he always seemed outwardly bursting with life and vigor. Yet I can remember meeting him with Mother at the Cedarhurst station on hot summer evenings and hugging him and feeling in the touch of his damp cheek that he was coming back to us, poor driven man, a hostage from the inexorable city that made a dull misery of the lives of men. And clinging to him, loving him, I felt that this would be my fate too and that it was a bond between us. How surprised he would have been! He who was so cheerful, so proud of his office, so anxious to buy me an ice cream cone before we drove home!

For neurotic reasons of my own, and probably in part because of the dominance of my mother in the home, a situation brought about much more by Father's wish than by any ambition on her part, I came to think of women as a privileged, happy lot, with the right to sit home all day on sofas and telephone, and of men as poor slaves doomed to go downtown and do dull, soul-breaking things to support their families. This was not the fault of women or men. It was simply the way things were. A woman was Cleopatra in the barge; a man, the galley slave. In brief enough time I, too, would be sent off to boarding school to learn the dusty task of being a man. Men were supposed to enjoy rough sports, but that was just a put-on, a cover-up, needed to keep the troops in line.

One day Father took me downtown to show me where he worked. He meant it to be fun. He got quite excited pointing out the buildings. There was Morgan's, there the Stock Exchange, there was Wall Street itself. Never shall I forget the horror inspired in me by those dark narrow streets and those tall sooty towers and by Trinity Church blocking the horizon with its black spire — a grim phallic symbol. When, years later, Father had his first crack-up, and it was blamed in part on his worry over an error in a trust indenture which might have (but did not) cost his firm millions, I felt a sad confirmation of my gloomiest anticipations.

Father and Mother were married when he was twenty-five and she twenty-three, after an engagement of two years. In the fifty-seven years of their union they were never parted except for a few days at a time in summers when Mother stayed with the children in Maine. They were so utterly devoted, so entirely intimate, that I always knew that one would tell the other anything I said. With this intimacy, however, went a great mutual respect and admiration. Even after Father's stroke, at eighty-two, when his mind was largely gone, Mother allowed him to mess up all his papers which I had carefully arranged. When I begged her to keep the desk drawer locked, she simply shook her head, murmuring: "Those are your father's papers." It was because of their closeness that I do not think that Mother ever really understood the extent to which she was the dominant partner. She thought of Father and herself as a unit. I didn't. I loved Father and deeply admired him, but he was a man. He went downtown to work with the other robots. Mother was real. I loved her too, but she was real.

I should state, to begin with, that Mother had eighty-three years of a good life. For a woman of her group and generation, it was also a successful life. She raised three sons: a lawyer-diplomat, a lawyer-writer, and a doctor; and a daughter who married an architect. She ran efficient households in three different places during the year; she was active on charitable committees; she was a quick and omnivorous reader. Her literary opinions were pungent, incisive, always interesting. And she specialized in people; she was an artist in friendship. She had an uncanny sense of the kernel in every human problem and would cut straight through to it with sympathy, with wit, with kindness. She was brisk, shrewd, humane, deep. She reserved the tale of her own troubles to a few intimates and family members and gave only the best of herself to her little public. There were times when I would complain to her that I wished I were not her son so that I could get more of that best.

But behind the impressive barricade of her personality lurked a constant state of fear. It was not fear for her own life. She died in full consciousness of impending death, tossing away mortality, in Emily Dickinson's phrase, "like a rind." It was a deep, inner fear that she, Priscilla, might somehow not do her duty in the eyes of undescried, murky gods and that the lives of her husband and children would be the forfeits. It was, of course, a neurosis, a kind of superstition, but it was so strong that I often marveled that it did not wreck her health.

Why? We never knew. For she was never psychoanalyzed. When she was six years old her baby brother became dangerously ill, and she remembered secretly hoping that he would die so that she could wear the smart mourning she had seen one of her older cousins wearing that season. But then the poor boy actually did die, and the appalled Priscilla learned from the sight of her grief-stricken parents what death really was. Had the guilt aroused by the memory of that childish lethal hope created a lasting neurosis? It easily could have. She and I often discussed it. But she never really believed that she needed psychiatric assistance. She once boasted to a psychoanalyst friend how well she had got on without the aid of his profession.

"Ah, but the woman you might have been!" he retorted.

That is the point. The woman she might have been. Hers was not a talent or a personality that should have been confined to a family and a handful of friends. Why not, the reader may demand, if she chose it that way? Because she did not choose it that way. She played the role in life that she felt she had to play. She cramped her natural personality to fit into the box that seemed always to be opening in front of her. This cramping process was all-important to me because I followed the example of her stronger personality. If she felt there were things one had to do to be a woman, then I, a moral copycat, had to feel there were things one had to do to be a man. But these things were dictated not by God or man or reason. They were dictated by fear.

Fear of what? It is hard to describe. Fear of a grading system in which one started with a handicap. Fear of not coming up to some kind of scratch. Fear of being measured in the balance and found wanting. I think it can be most closely likened to the fear created in primitive man by his sense of the tribe. Mother was never afraid of people; she was devoid of worldly ambition and snobbishness, but she always had the deepest respect for conventions, even for fetishes. She seemed to feel that she had to live up to all the standards of the tribe — more so than others, for she was under some malign disfavor — but that if she did so, if she was humble and conscientious and good, then the tribe would bear her up, sustain her, protect her and hers from danger. And what was the tribe? Presumably it took different forms at different times. It might have been all those uncles and aunts in "Dixon Alley." It might have been the partners in Father's law firm, or those of its principal banking client, J. P. Morgan & Co. It might have been brownstone New York itself, or the eastern financial establishment, or, in the last analysis, America the beautiful. For Mother, in her emotional moments, could be arrantly sentimental.

Of course, I am speaking of the deepest emotions, the id. Mother was capable of looking at facts very clearly indeed and even at such speculations as have been made in this chapter. But her intellect, particularly when I was growing up, was constantly summoned to the task of "dressing up" the tribe and the tribal deities. She had a natural disinclination to be kicked around by gods who were unworthy of her. Like a Greek of ancient days, who might have wished to draw a veil over the amorous activities of Zeus, so Mother tried to see the Dixon family as the ultimate in loyalty and love, Father's partners as idealistic priests of the law, the Morgan bankers as revered symbols of financial wisdom and integrity. She showed a Victorian seriousness in her need to see all the fundamentals of her life and surroundings as morally sound.

My trouble with Mother's evaluations came early. The difficulty was that we lived so uninterruptedly and in such close quarters with the social fabric to which she attached these admirable qualities that I could not help but observe how much more often than not these were lacking. Had my parents sent me to a public school, or even to some private boarding institution in the South or Middle West, had they elected to spend at least their summers away from their own social world, I might have been able to ignore the accuracy or inaccuracy of Mother's classifications. But as it was, I was kept with my nose at all times pressed to the pane through which I observed with her the same environment. The family routine of winters in Manhattan and summers at fashionable watering places was never varied while I was little. Nor was the daily club life at Bar Harbor ever interrupted by a camp or camping trip or sailing cruise or even a summer job. Until I was adult I never spent a single night out-of-doors.

Now why was this? What made a woman as serious and intelligent as my mother go in so intensely for such frivolous communities? One answer is that she had grown up in them herself and that she always had a strong faith in familiar scenes. The unknown, the woods, the wilderness, the sea were for her full of images of sudden death for her offspring. Who could be hurt on a tennis court or a golf course or in a swimming pool? The summer colonies were tested and true. Secondly, Mother actually liked the huddled aspect of watering places. She loved her sense of the tribe all around and close by. She was as public a person as Louis XIV and would have been perfectly happy at Versailles. Mother could not even comprehend the need in others for privacy, or why as children we resented her opening our mail. Her idea of the most wonderful thing in the world was a large, close, constantly united family, and in her later years she would deplore what she deemed the idle concern with overpopulation, pointing to the meager park lands along the highways leading into New York City as proof that there was plenty of space for more human beings. It was her one irrationality.

Finally, Mother and Father did not see how the silly side of fashionable summer life could do their children any real harm. They found the worthy people in Maine and Long Island so worthy and the silly social types so utterly ridiculous, that they did not for a long time fathom that a child might not agree with them. Strong in their own innate decency, in their own high moral standards, they saw no reason why they could not live out a pastoral idyll in the very heart of Sodom or Gomorrah.

But I did not even want to be uncontaminated. I observed that often the only interesting thing about some of the families near whom we lived was their wealth. I saw perfectly that their big houses, their shining cars, and their glittering yachts were designed to impress just such onlookers as myself. And I began to see that there was diversion and interest in the rivalries of the social game. When I bubbled over at the family board with snobbish observations and gossip about our wealthy neighbors, Mother and Father were genuinely astounded and depressed. It became a rather sour family joke that I had inherited the characteristics of Mother's paternal grandmother, a comic legend in the family for the naiveté of her worldly values. "Don't speak ill of Mrs. Kingsland," she had told a grandchild; "she has three million dollars." But although I felt guilty at being so detected (for I always believed that Mother had to be fundamentally right), I yet began to develop a resentment at the curious life we led. If we could never play the social game, what in God's name were we doing in Bar Harbor?

And after Bar Harbor what? I shuddered at the future that my parents seemed to offer. The happiness of life, according to them, or according to my perverse interpretation of their philosophy, would consist in undergoing the strain and boredom of an overworked downtown existence in order to provide funds for the large noisy family whose function in turn was to provide solace and consolation for the father who was giving up his life for it. I found the idea as stifling as a hot blanket on a summer day. If money had to be made, would it not be better to come by a large hunk of it and spend it for all the glittering things that Bar Harbor and Long Island offered? When all was said and done, were not the silliest creatures under the umbrella tables at the Bar Harbor Swimming Club having a better time than Mother and Father?

Years before I dared to speculate that I might do anything as different as becoming a writer, I was beginning to see my family and their friends in terms of stories. In fierce rejection of what I took as Mother's cloying concept of swaddled domesticity and Father's disingenuous estimate that we were a typical middle-class family, I sought all the drama I could find in the wealth and greed that surrounded us. I enthusiastically noted which were the richest cousins, which the richest ancestors; I counted divorces and infidelities in the family tree with glee; I strained for foreign titles and financial scandals. Oh, if I was going to be vulgar, I had to be the most vulgar of all! But at least I might live.

The irony was that the person who told me the best stories, who gave me the most dramatic information, was Mother herself. Her idealism found its outlet in generalities. In particulars, with individuals, she could see every stain and wart. She was a chest of information on New York families, particularly her own, and she was endlessly amusing, endlessly interesting. It was not only the woman she might have been that I regret. It was the writer.

And so the ambivalence in me was born; the sense that the world was packed with drama and the warning sense at the same time that this drama was not a thing that could be used. It was all right for the home, for gossip by the fireside, for the humorous give-and-take of cozy family life. But beyond that family life there was another life — for men. That life, however dull, however deadly, was brave and earnest. It was a lawyer's life, a banker's, even a doctor's. And all the things that were fun were like the dirty things that one did alone when one closed the bathroom door, the sound of which caused Mother immediately to prick up suspicious ears.

BOVEE IDYLL

THE BOVEE SCHOOL for boys occupied a remodeled brownstone on Fifth Avenue just south of 65th Street. It faced the Arsenal Building and the Central Park Zoo. At recess, crossing the Avenue to exercise in the park, we would march in twos past the cages but were never allowed to stop. The noisy destruction of the great French Renaissance palace which Richard Morris Hunt had reared for the Astors on the north corner of 65th Street helped to develop my early sense of the transiency of city landmarks.

Private schools in New York in the 1920s were the private property of their headmasters or headmistresses, and this was the source of both the glory and the decline of Bovee. Miss Kate Bovee, the founder, had raised the school to the rank of Buckley and St. Bernard's, among the first in Manhattan. In 1924, the last year of her life, she was a distant, rather terrifying creature to a first grader, with a reputation for hurling books at inattentive boys. But with her death, a prompt decadence set in. Her younger sister Eleanor ran the school which she had inherited for five years of accelerating decline until she had the foresight to sell the valuable lot on which it was situated just before the 1929 crash and retire to Italy. The unfortunate faculty were flung out of work, in which plight they were soon to find millions of companions.

"Miss Eleanor," as she was known, was a goose. She directed academic affairs from an office that was furnished like a living room with chairs and sofas upholstered in deep blue and photographs of Roman ruins and villas. She had a lofty soul and high aesthetic ideals, and the crudity of boys was a source of constant disillusionment to her. She offered a prize which she called the "Noble Life Prize" to the boy who had led the "noblest life" each year. I remember how we chuckled one commencement day when she handed it, dewy-eyed, to an eighth grader of notoriously dirty talk and habits.

Miss Eleanor's faith in badges threatened to turn the school into a mint. For a year of perfect attendance and punctuality one received a gold medal. For a year of such perfection marred only by illness, one received a silver medal. For a year marred only by illness or lateness of arrival on Monday mornings caused by the drive into town against traffic after a country weekend, one received a bronze medal. Three years of a gold medal culminated in a gold watch; three of a baser medal in a watch of that metal. Two years of gold and one of silver were rewarded with a gold watch with silver trimmings; two of gold and one of bronze . . . but there was no end to it. It is small wonder that my mother, to my great indignation, kept me home arbitrarily for one day at the beginning of each school year to disqualify me at the outset for either medal or watch. But at least thereafter we lived in peace, free of the daily panic of being late for school.

I was happy at Bovee. It had a pleasant, relaxed atmosphere, with none of the grimness that I already associated with boarding schools. One was free of the danger of hazing and physical harassment from other boys, for we were always either in classrooms or in supervised groups in the park. Oddly enough, whereas in boarding school boys were apt to be assaulted only by their peers, never by the faculty, at Bovee the custom was just the opposite. There the masters would pull our hair, each in his characteristic way. Mr. Sedgwick, a dainty man, would take a small lock and twist it tightly; Mr. Lockman, a huge choleric type, would grab a fistful and shake until one's teeth rattled. But it never hurt very much, and we took it mostly in good part. The lady teachers, of course, never touched us at all.

I think one reason that Bovee was amiable was that it had a broader mix than some of the other private schools. It had many Jewish boys as well as sons of artists and writers. My own class produced two famous actors: Mel Ferrer and Efrem Zimbalist, Jr. Such a thing would have been considered a miracle at Buckley, and not a desirable one, either. Bovee may have been disintegrating under Miss Eleanor, but it was free of the deadly dryness that afflicts anti-Jewish institutions in largely Jewish communities.

Like other children, I took the anti-Semitism which then characterized the Protestant society of New York for granted. Most of the schools and clubs admitted no Jews at all unless they were converted or unless they had married Christians. Brearley was considered "liberal" because it took one Jewish girl per class. Yet I can never recall thinking that my parents or their friends had any particular animus against Jews. Their attitude was simply another arbitrary "grown-up" thing. I knew that the Jewish boys at Bovee could not be members of our country club, but since I loathed all country clubs, it did not occur to me that they would much mind. I can even remember explaining to cousins at a Christmas party that Father had sold our house in Cedarhurst because Cedarhurst had become "too Jewish," and this being accepted as impassively as if I had spoken of the pollution of air by a factory. I suspect that the lack of emotion connected with this prejudice may have been the reason that it was so easy for me and most of my contemporaries to drop it altogether when we grew up.

The same thing may be said about the prejudice against Roman Catholics. This certainly existed, though, like the anti-Semitism, it was snobbish rather than religious in nature. Catholicism was associated in our minds with the poor, ignorant Irish maids who worked such long hours and slept in often unheated areas on the top of brownstone houses. So far as blacks were concerned, however, there was no prejudice at all, because blacks did not exist for us. Nobody that I knew even had a black servant. They lived up in Harlem, presumably because they liked it, and our paths never crossed. If any particularly dreadful fact of poverty or discrimination was impressed upon us, I think our attitude was probably that we had fought a war to free them and that that should be enough.

What I recall as most exciting in Bovee was feeling for the first time sophisticated. By sophistication I mean having opinions about people and things quite other than what my family held. I developed a tiny clique of close, gossipy friends, and we happily made scathing remarks about the more popular boys and teachers, even using a code in which we exchanged uncomplimentary messages in classrooms. The world of the movies, too, began to be opened to us, and we were in giggling ecstasies over Corinne Griffith in *The Divine Lady* or Dolores del Rio in *Ramona*. My mother allowed me to go only rarely, but I learned eagerly from the others what they had seen and deemed myself badly treated.

I was bored by athletics, but this did not matter because there was so little demanded of one at Bovee. I had to play soccer, it was true, on occasional afternoons in Central Park, but I was so clumsy that I was usually relegated to the bench where I could gaze south and west at the great towers that lined the park and daydream of a fantastic future (not really believed in) beyond boys, beyond boarding school, beyond

32

family, a future that might be a pastiche of all the films I had seen or heard about. It was a happy, idle combination of wanting to grow up and wanting to grow up as a child.

My Peter Pan of this period was a boy called Tommy Curtiss. He had a good deal more latitude than I, for his mother allowed him to go to the movies whenever he wanted and even, occasionally, to a musical comedy, and had a red Rolls-Royce in which to transport him. He has maintained his interest in films and recently published a biography of Erich von Stroheim. My mother did not at all approve of Tommy who at twelve was reading *The Well of Loneliness* and whose family's chauffeur dropped me home from school in the red Rolls that I wanted all the block to see. But there was not very much she could do about it except take me out of Bovee. When she tried this, protesting that the school was obviously going to pieces, I fought her so bitterly that she abandoned the idea. When my younger brother, Howland, went to school, however, he was sent to Allen-Stevenson.

Bovee was only one of the institutions that claimed my busy days. There was Mrs. Hubbell's Dancing Class which met on Thursday afternoons in the ballroom of the Colony Club. Mrs. Hubbell was a great stiff column of a woman decorated each week in a different variety of silk or satin but always surmounted by the capital of a Queen Mary hat. Perhaps she had learned the style at first hand, for it was rumored that she had instructed the Princess Royal. My nurse, Maggie, like most of the nurses, was enormously impressed by Mrs. Hubbell. Although the latter seemed the very symbol of an established past, she was capable of a royal nod to the present, for she condescended to have us given lessons by an assistant in the Charleston and even in tap dancing. As a preparation for the former she made us all stand about her in a solemn circle to practice slowly bending our knees. If anything could have less suggested the vivacity of the dance itself, she probably would

33

have used it. The tap dance instructor invited us all to ask our parents to have clogs attached to our patent leather shoes, and I had a terrible time persuading Mother to allow this. What with movies and Noble Life medals, tap dancing with clogs and a friend who read *The Well of Loneliness*, she must have yearned for the day when I could be sent away to Groton.

There were the arts of war to be learned as well as those of the ballroom. Miss Eleanor, to prepare us to defend our country, invited a Major Smith to come to Bovee at recess. He kept us away from the park and trained us to stand absolutely still for minutes at a time without moving a muscle. We all abominated Major Smith, but I was soon to fall even more closely under his jurisdiction, for at the age of eleven I was enrolled in the Knickerbocker Grays of which he was director. For two afternoons a week I and a couple of hundred other boys, dressed in gray uniforms, learned close order drill in the Park Avenue Armory. I remember protesting to Mother the impropriety of having to get into the Madison Avenue trolley in full uniform accompanied by a nurse. But the argument of a later era — "old enough to fight, old enough to vote" — had not then been heard of.

My year in the Grays ended in a mock battle. My battalion was to storm a cannon, and at a certain point in the exercise we were to lie down on the floor to indicate our total annihilation. It seemed to me that a touch of drama was needed. What else was the good of the movies? Before extending my length on the boards, I swayed, I staggered, I clutched at my chest and finally pitched forward as Ramon Novarro might have done. This performance was observed with great disgust by an older cousin who gloried in a lieutenant's plume. It was the last gesture of poetry before the advent of boarding school.

THE RECTOR OF GROTON

When i wrote *The Rector of Justin* I was trying to paint the portrait of a headmaster of a New England boarding school who would be characteristic of the great era of headmasters which began, roughly speaking, at the end of the last century and ended some time before World War II. It was the era which produced Endicott Peabody of Groton, Samuel Drury of St. Paul's, William Thayer of St. Mark's, Mather Abbott of Lawrenceville, and many others. I read all the privately printed biographies (a dreary lot) and made notes of what I deduced to be the salient characteristics of their subjects. But when I came to put my man together, I cast him in part in the mold of a non-teacher: Judge Learned Hand, the greatest human being that it has ever been my privilege to know. I tried to make my headmaster a man of giant intellect, of passionate idealism, of searing doubts, of mordant humor. All this, of course, availed me nothing with the Groton School alumni who took for granted, because certain facts and dates had been borrowed from the life of Endicott Peabody, that Peabody was the rector of Justin. Readers of fiction go purely by externals in seeking the human models for characters in novels. Put Hitler in a white gown with a Leonardo hairdo, and they will swear he is Jesus Christ.

What particularly intrigued me about this willful identification of Peabody with my hero was that the two characters were near opposites. My Francis Prescott was complex, arrogant, witty, cynical, intellectual to his fingertips; Peabody was simple, straightforward, literal, and always sincere. Prescott was a bit of a charlatan, a bit of a chameleon. Peabody seemed eternally the same, true as steel. And, finally, Peabody always struck me as a man who must have *looked* the same to everyone — however differently they might evaluate him.

He had hovered over my childhood, long before I went to Groton. My father, like the fathers of most of my form mates, had gone to the school and held him in deep reverence. There had never been any idea of my not going to Groton. No later than the age of twelve I was certain to come under the jurisdiction of this huge, magnificent old man whose cheerful greetings to my family when encountered during a Mount Desert Island summer never fooled me for a minute about the ultimate hardships of his strict disciplinary academy in cold New England winters. I knew that such things had to be. If one had to endure homesickness and hazing and snowballs, if one had to take ice-cold showers and play rough sports, it was part of the indoctrination required of my sex. Left at home with Mother in a woman's world of cushions and caresses, one would turn into a sissy, and that was to be damned. Such was my grim, self-imposed, childhood creed. It lacked only a deity when I went to Groton in the fall of 1929. Dr. Peabody filled that role as air fills a vacuum.

We had not been without religion at home. Neither of my parents was ever much of a believer, but we had been exposed to Sunday services, both Episcopalian and Presbyterian, and the beautiful, mellifluous sermons of Albert Parker Fitch (a part-time novelist) at the Park Avenue Presbyterian Church had delighted me. But I had very little real faith of any kind before I went to Groton. There the combination of my misery and loneliness with my bedazzlement by the awesome figure of the headmaster produced a state of brief but intense religiosity. I used afterwards to think of this period of my life as a kind of dark ages. I was a monk in a day of warring barbarians, but I always had a cross and a stained glass window before my reverent eyes.

The important part of this to my story was that the rector — or my distortion of him — seemed to prove out what my parents had only vaguely postulated. They had been like crude but honest heralds whose garbled message was thunderously justified by the coming of the Messiah. However anxious, however even boldly inclined I might have been to argue with them that the world of Bovee and Tommy Curtiss had at least a quasi validity, I could only now submit to the crushing proof that, if my parents had seen through a glass darkly, we were at last face to face!

Endicott Peabody had (he was then in his seventies) "command presence" as I have never seen it since, not even in four years of overseas duty in World War II. He was a very large man, with big hands and muscles, a square countenance, a mostly bald head, and a Roman nose dominated by gray eyes which were capable of the sternest, glassiest stare that I have ever beheld. He moved jerkily, but this was from age. As a young man he had been a good athlete, and he played handball (or what we called "fives") into his eighties. When he laughed, his eyes became almost tender, and one could feel a great pull of affection toward him, but when he reprimanded, he was simply terrifying, like God in a Blake watercolor.

Groton School was everything to him. He had founded it, built it, nurtured it. He was present in every brick, in the soapstone basins of the lavatories, in the gleaming white columns of the porches, in the square, stout, uncompromising tower of the chapel. I know that he loved his family, but I am sure that they always came second to the school. For to him the school was sacred; it was a temple designed to keep boys unspotted from the world until such time as they should have developed the moral strength to cope triumphantly with that world. Nothing that went on on the campus — in the kitchens, in the cellars, in the infirmary, as well as in the classrooms and on the playing fields — was beneath the rector's notice. Like Napoleon, he never really delegated. He did everything himself, and his staff, from the senior master to the humblest kitchen maid, merely helped him in his great task.

The rector was essentially a simple man with one gigantic preoccupation: his mission to prepare boys to receive Christ. He had a never-sleeping sense of imminent corruption lurking in idleness, in tobacco, in alcohol, in loose women, and in something that he darkly defined as "sentimentality" which presumably embraced all forms of pederasty, physical or sublimated. Certain activities were freer than others of the dangers of corruption: sports, drills, community singing, hard work of almost any kind, family life, clean joking. Other interests were permissible provided an alert eye was always kept to see that they did not slip over into gushiness: music, painting, reading, writing, indulgence generally in the arts, either creatively or passively. But I do not think that the rector ever really believed that the arts were quite worth the risk. He would have scorned to have been the author of *Hamlet* or the painter of the Sistine Chapel had such feats entailed responsibility for the "sentimental" sonnets of Shakespeare or of Michelangelo.

Yet there was one area in which "gushiness" could be excused — or almost. That was in religion. The rector had a near-mystic side of his nature. He used to pray in chapel, quite without self-consciousness, his eyes closed, his voice at times shaking. His sermons, which were poorly organized and lacking in spark, nonetheless had a certain force which they owed to their delivery. As the rector aged his sermons tended to fuse into one, repeated over and over, an odd pastiche of all his favorite quotations and anecdotes. What gave it such value as it had was the passion of the preacher who, when he had made a point, would wave his robed arm violently up and down crying: "That's it, boys! That's it!"

Now the essential observation that I want to make about this remarkable man was that he was at all times simple, direct, and totally consistent in the pursuit of his goal. Given his premise — that fathers, sons, and ultimately grandsons would benefit spiritually by spending the years from twelve to seventeen in a vigorously athletic cloister with the cross constantly before their eyes — everything else follows. Why was Groton made up of rich, eastern families? Because being a family school, it had to keep on with the families which had started it. Why, then, did it start with the rich? Because who else in 1881 was going to support a new school started by three young men? Was it not only natural for Peabody to go to his Boston business connections for financial backing? But why were there no Jews, almost no Catholics? Because a Protestant Episcopal Church School naturally excluded other faiths. Why, then, were there no converted Jews? Because the rector suspected that their conversion sprang from motives of social ambition.

And so it went. What it was almost impossible for outsiders to believe was that the rector was sincere about all this. Yet he was. He had little respect for birth or wealth. He was not a snob. He was not intolerant of other faiths. I believe that he thought one was more apt to find a "gentleman" in the best sense of that dangerous word among upper-middle-class Bostonians than among Irish or Italian immigrants, but he would have been most unusual in his generation had he not. And he certainly believed that his church was the surest route to God. Yet he never claimed to have all the answers. He claimed only to have all the answers at Groton. Because Groton was his. He had made it.

He devoted each waking hour to his task. He could be very agreeable, very funny, at a social gathering; he could be charming to school visitors; he could be instructive and interesting about current events. But these things were mere veils over the great rock of his constant concentration on his school and the presence of God in it. He never digressed for long. His eye would fall upon an untied tie, on an unclosed locker, on two boys whispering in chapel or assembly; it would note the absence of a master from table, or a cloud that threatened the football match. I have compared him to Napoleon. Louis XIV offers an even more apt analogy. The court at Versailles was the Sun King's creation and total preoccupation. He noticed when a duke was absent or if a taboret were occupied by a lady of insufficient rank. Like the rector, he believed that his system would work only if he were constantly vigilant. Both were correct.

If the rector was worshiped, he was also much resented. It was unbearable to many to concede that such a school, run by such a man, could succeed at all. It had to be a tenet of these critics that the rector was a snob and a bigot and that Groton was a repudiation of every natural and normal impulse in a man. I subsequently learned some sympathy with the latter part of this point of view. But at the time I regarded the whole of it as simple heresy. "I can forgive you, but I wonder if God can," the rector was reputed to have said to an erring graduate. "If you can forgive me, sir," the graduate was said to have replied, "I am sure God can." That was how I felt. I even tried to imprint my amoebic personality on those glassy eyeballs. I would go to the rector after confirmation class with trumped-up questions about sanitation and the common use of the communion cup, or the descent into hell, and would be secretly shamed by the grave care and attention that he gave to my factitious doubts. Whatever you said or thought about Endicott Peabody, he always ended up by being bigger than you.

Of course, I did not really think he was God, or even a manifestation of God. I was a sensible, orthodox Episcopalian. God, after all, knew my innermost thoughts, and the rector did not. I was sure he did not, for he would have thrown me out of Groton if he had, along with all the other boys. For didn't we have obscene, heretical, even "sentimental" thoughts? Didn't the rector himself, maybe? Just maybe? No! On that I was perfectly clear. The rector never had dirty thoughts and never *had* had them. When I say that there is a part of me that still believes that, the reader may get a sense of the impact of this man.

GROTON

THE GROTON CAMPUS struck even me as beautiful on the September day in 1929 when I first saw it, just two weeks before my twelfth birthday. The horrid, sinking feeling of saying good-bye to Mother was succeeded by a sense of mild curiosity and of faint, nervous relief. Some of the other first formers introduced themselves to me quite politely. I enjoyed my new clothes, my new hairbrushes and toilet articles. My dormitory master, Mr. Gallien, was all charm, and my brother John, a sixth former, the soul of tact and consideration. Perhaps the gods had been placated. Perhaps Groton would be almost endurable.

But those first two weeks were a brief euphoria. One mild, clear Saturday afternoon I walked with two other boys to Groton Village which we were allowed to visit once a week to buy candy and ice cream. Crossing a railroad bridge, we paused to look down at the track. Suddenly we heard a whistle; a freight train was approaching. As it roared underneath the bridge, engulfing us in a cloud of smoke, we hurled pebbles down on the roofs of the cars — at least on what we thought were the roofs of the cars.

The following Monday morning the first form met for its class in sacred studies under the aegis of the headmaster. The rector used this course as a way to get to know the new boys, whose names he never thereafter forgot. He made a great point of a curious union of personal sanitation with preparedness for work by calling out: "Nails and notebooks!" at which injunction we would submit our fingernails for his personal inspection and then hold up our copybooks as evidence that we were ready to inscribe his precepts. But that morning he commenced with a grave announcement. The engineer of a local train had called to complain that the window of his locomotive had been smashed by a rock the previous Saturday afternoon and that he had narrowly escaped injury. He accused Groton boys of the crime. The rector assured us that he doubted very much that any of his boys could have been guilty of such lawlessness, but he had promised the indignant man that all classes would be interrogated. Did any of us know anything about it?

I rose to my feet in what I recall as a totally reflex action.

"I did it, sir."

The great staring eyes were severe, but they were also distinctly surprised.

"You did? Were there any other boys with you?"

"Yes, sir. Biddle and Bigelow were with me."

It no more occurred to me to withhold these names than it would occur to a resurrected body to equivocate with Jehovah on the Day of Judgment. But that was my fatal error. Punishment for the stone throwing amounted only to a few hours' work on the next two Saturday afternoons and a trip to the village station to apologize to the angry engineer. But punishment for telling on Biddle and Bigelow amounted to a whole season of purgatory.

That same day, at recess, I was surrounded by a mob yelling "Snitcher!" Although at Bovee I had not been indoctrinated into any code of schoolboy honor, ignorance of the law proved no excuse. Anyway, the persecution that followed long outlasted the memory of my breach of etiquette. It turned on me personally. For I was naturally unpopular. I was a hopeless athlete. I was bored by most of the things that interested other boys and naive enough not to conceal my boredom. I was timid, affected, and fastidious. I even got bad marks. By every schoolboy standard I was an unlovely and useless thing. The others would have found me out in time even without the snitching.

The terrible thing about unpopularity in a school of those days was the unremitting way in which it was flung in one's face. There were no afternoons or weekends off. There was no absenting oneself from the campus. There was no way, day or night, to be free of one's tormenters. I do not claim that I had my books kicked out of my hand every time I came around a corner, or that I had my face pushed in the mud or snow every time I went outside, but I learned to be relieved when such things did *not* occur. And then there were the sneers, the insults, the vicious, never-ending nicknames. In class, at night, in chapel, I was constantly assaulted with them, in shouts or songs or whispers. And there was never a friend to intervene, for, by definition, I had no friends.

Oh, yes, the faculty were kind and well-meaning. They knew I was wretched, but what could they do? One night, at a party in the dormitory, I was pelted from head to foot with ice cream, and in the general scuffle I lost my bite plate. I knew this had cost a hundred dollars, which seemed to me a great sum for my parents to be out, and for the first time I burst into tears. Mr. Gallien arrived, sent my enemies flying, put his arm around my heaving shoulders, and asked me what the trouble was. When I explained, he went down on his hands and knees and searched until he found the bite plate. I was undone by such kindness and sobbed bitterly. Never to this day have I forgotten my deep gratitude to that good man, but even then I was faintly embarrassed for him. One didn't show such kindness to the victims of the gods.

When, long years afterwards, I wrote a story about a school persecution called "Billy and the Gargoyles," my friend Malcolm Strachan, then a teacher at Groton, told me that what had most appalled him about it was that the boy *approved* of his own persecution. That was indeed the real horror. Had the experience inspired a noble rebellion . . . ah, well. But it didn't. I was like those victims in Nazi prison camps who, brainwashed, clutched and kissed the hands of their guards. For I, too, believed in the Groton system. Had not I always known things would be thus?

One may wonder why, so many years after Freud's discoveries, my parents thought it was a healthy thing for a child to live through such a long period of vilification. Was it good for me to be universally labeled an effeminate moron, a non-male, a repulsive, unsexed creature, all day, every day, for months? The answer is that they never knew. Mother suspected that things were not going well for me at Groton. She came up to school and told me that if I was unhappy, she would take me out. And she meant it, too. But I was scandalized and actually frightened at the prospect of such a defeat. How could one explain to a privileged woman what a man's doom was? I promised her that all was well, and I was relieved when she went away, distressed and perplexed.

Did this kind of treatment of a boy make for success in later life? There are those who claim that the brutalities of the British public school helped build the British empire. But was that altogether a good thing? From the twenty-nine boys in my form who graduated in 1935 we produced a secretary of the army, an assistant secretary of state, presidents of the First National City Bank, the Mellon Bank, and the Celanese Corporation, ambassadors to the Philippines and to Indonesia, a novelist, a Benedictine monk, some eminent lawyers and doctors, no failures — in a worldly sense. Perhaps they would have all done as well coming from other schools. How can one tell? All I can state is my personal belief that hazing accomplishes as much good as burning witches. And, of course, there is another side to the argument. Groton did not seem nearly as tough to everybody as it did to me. One of the boys in our form who became a major executive told me that he had been severely handicapped in business by Groton standards of good manners and fair play. Yet even he admitted that his most ruthless competitor had been another "Grotty."

My persecution ebbed at last, and I experienced the bliss of simple neglect. Even today I find it a bit difficult to comprehend the modern terror of loneliness. I now developed an entrancing new interest, my health. I had a series of hacking colds which kept me in the infirmary, a sanctuary as sure as a church in the Middle Ages. I soon learned how to touch my thermometer to a lamp bulb to keep my temperature above the fatal 98.6 which signaled one's return to the outside world. Once I went too far and stuck the thermometer in the spout of the nurse's coffeepot. The zinc broke off! When I heard her brisk step approaching down the corridor, I recalled with horror that zinc could be poisonous. It was better to be bawled out for clumsiness than hanged for murder so I swept the pot to the floor with a crash as she turned the corner and pleaded to her outraged countenance that I had stumbled against it.

Eventually I was sent home for a tonsillectomy, and I enjoyed dull blank peaceful days of further reprieve. Bovee School had been dissolved, and the faculty were largely unemployed. Mother hired my favorite master, Mr. Evans, a gentle, patient, scholarly soul, to tutor me. She always arranged that he should take lunch at the penthouse apartment to which we had rashly moved just before the crash, so that he could count on one good meal that day. We were living in the spring of 1930. For the first time it occurred to my preoccupied mind that there might be troubles off the Groton campus.

By second-form year life at Groton was considerably more tranquil, and I even had one or two friends, pariahs like myself. But now trouble came, not from the boys, but from the faculty. My marks, always low, hit bottom, the result of poor training at Bovee and the school time missed in tonsillitis. Yet even so, my general average might not have placed me in danger of being dropped a form (the most hideous of all disgraces and one that added another long year to the eternity of the Groton sentence) had it not been for the zeros that I obtained for my daily recitations in Latin which made my line in Mr. De Veau's grade book appear, as he mockingly put it, "like a chain across the page."

Fritz De Veau, a well-to-do bachelor, an ex-lawyer, and a man of considerable charm in the world of adults, was also a cynic, a strange thing to find on Dr. Peabody's faculty. His devotion to the rector, however, was total. Except for his feeling for Latin prose and poetry, and a certain talent for friendship, which I was later in life to appreciate, it was his only noticeable sentiment. His value to Groton was that he was the only master (and there should always be one) who treated boys entirely as if they were grown-ups. This was keenly appreciated by the more sophisticated of the fifth and sixth forms, but to their juniors he was at best an iceberg, at worst a monster. If he believed that a boy was intelligent, he could imagine no excuse for a poor performance. I was lazy, and that was that.

I became hypnotized by my horrible record in Latin class. Each time that Mr. De Veau called on me, my mind would close up, and I would await in dumb misery the inevitable, invariable dry comment: "Another goose egg, Auchincloss." But in my desperation, for the first time I managed not to be entirely passive. I began to look about for a solution. There were two divisions of Latin in my form, and I was in the "A"

47

division, although my abysmal marks seemed to shout for a "B" classification. I was kept in "A" only because of Mr. De Veau's insistence that I was not using my capacity. I decided that if I could only arrange to be transferred to "B" Latin, I might be able to save myself.

When Mother came up, I put this to her. She went to Fritz De Veau, whom she knew and liked (he was a popular "extra man" in Bar Harbor), but he argued that I was only trying to get out of a little hard work. Mother then went to the rector who, of course, backed up De Veau. "But can't we at least try it Louis's way?" she insisted. The rector at last agreed.

I knew that I had displayed hubris in interfering with such fundamental concerns, and I knew that I would have to make good. When I reported to Second "B" Latin, Mr. Andrews, who had graduated to the faculty after being for years the rector's secretary, the dearest and plainest of old men with a great purple birthmark over one temple, showed unwonted severity. "We hear you've come down here because you don't want to work," he announced to me before the class. "Well, we'll have an eye on you." I didn't care. I loved Mr. Andrews. I had hope in my heart. And in only a few weeks' time he was beaming at me. There were no more goose eggs across the page.

From now on my life was a different thing. I had a key at last that fitted the Groton lock, the key of marks. I was not such an ass as to kid myself that it was a key to popularity or to leadership, like personal charm or athletic prowess. But I saw that it was the key to respectability and that respectability could lead to success. For to be successful in the world one did not have to be either popular or a leader. Everyone knew that "tycoons" were often small, ugly, unamiable men. I did not exactly visualize myself becoming a tycoon, but I cherished the idea of unlikely predominances, and I thought of myself as a priest in medieval times using the church as a way to bypass birth and brawn. My fantasies now were all of persons in power despite some handicap: Mowgli, a naked boy, leading the wolf pack; Queen Elizabeth, an aged virgin dominating a court of warriors; Richelieu, a red-robed invalid holding the French nobility at bay. In only two more years I was to be thrilled by the sirens of FDR's police escort as the presidential cortege roared into the Groton campus. The mighty man was a cripple!

But I had to work. For the next three years marks were everything to me. I sought permission to rise before the waking bell so that I could study. I would fib outrageously, and without a qualm, in stating on the "physical exercise blanks" that I had done the required sports and then hide away on winter afternoons to do my Latin or mathematics. My marks rose steadily, astoundingly. I moved into all "A" divisions. In time I was again under De Veau, but now we got on famously. I became first in my form. I even once became first in the school. The rector used to read aloud the monthly averages at assembly, and it was the custom to applaud those which were over 90 — there were rarely more than two or three. Never shall I forget the sweet sound of those clapping hands! I thought my heart would burst.

Needless to say, my parents were soon alarmed. They saw that the cure threatened to be worse than the disease. Mother actually offered me a money bribe to drop my average. Could anything, I thought indignantly as I spurned her lure, more clearly prove that women, the privileged class, did not even understand the conditions of the workers? Not since Marie Antoinette had directed the poor to the pâtisserie had there been such evidence of female frivolity in the presence of serious things.

The parental assault, however, may have generated some inner sense that I was unduly restricting myself, even in the interests of my own ambition. It was the custom at Groton for the graduating sixth form to publish a yearbook in which, beside the photograph of each member, were listed the accomplishments of his extracurricular career. The rules on which activities qualified for such mention were fairly relaxed, and a career could be saved from the creamy blankness of the book's expensive paper by even so slight an office as "rober in chapel to the rector," but it still behooved me to give the matter some consideration, for no mention at all was accorded to grades or academic prizes. Ultimately, I decided to work for the *Grotonian*, the school magazine, and for the dramatic society, the activities most closely linked to academe. I did not wish to "waste" an ounce of energy.

My writing had already begun in English class, again entirely for grades. A short story about the horrors of the September Massacres in the French Revolution had marked my debut in print in *The Third Form Weekly*. It had been followed with a tale about Nero's matricide. The next year I had written two lengthy unpublished and unpublishable pieces for "extra credit" in English. One of these was about children who went back into the past, heavily inspired by E. Nesbit's *The House of Arden* which Mother had read aloud to me years before. The other was a turgid "epic" poem in blank verse, again about the French Revolution but in particular about the sad fate of the Queen. It was entitled "Fallen Majesty" and showed a seventeenth-century fondness for abstract nouns and adjectives. I remember Mr. Gallien pointing out that the tumbrel which carried my unhappy heroine to her execution might have been insufficiently identified as a "repulsive vehicle."

The first stories of mine which were disassociated from English composition requirements were written directly for the *Grotonian*. By fifth-form year I was a regular contributor; by sixth I was chief editor. Every one of these pieces was written solely for the magazine, and I would have deemed them a total waste of time if they had not been printed. None of them, in other words, had been written for *me*, or to work out any particular inner problem of mine. None of them represented any compulsion on my part to express myself. They were devoid of subtlety, routinely sentimental. Their subjects were drawn from the world of my vacations: the swimming club of Bar Harbor, the Metropolitan Opera House, the gardens at Versailles. This may sound personal enough, but it wasn't. "Personal" would have been life at Groton.

Perhaps that is why these stories, read today, seem feeble even for a schoolboy. They show no promise. Of course, I give those critics who see in my work only a superfluous echo of John P. Marquand a wonderful opening: they show no promise because there was no promise. But what I mean is that they show no promise that their author would even one day be a professional writer. For they were not genuine literary efforts. They were simply an adjunct to my violent campaign for high marks and personal distinction.

As a sixth former I was at last thoroughly happy at Groton. I had made a place for myself in the school. I was editor in chief of the magazine and president of the Dramatic Society, a figure to be reckoned with on that tiny campus. I had plenty of friends now. Of course, I enjoyed no real popularity or leadership. I was not a prefect of the school or a member of any varsity team. But these things I had long discounted. Indeed I reveled in a perverse sense of superiority. I took positive pleasure in *not* attending the principal athletic events. I opposed a hard crust of intellectual and social snobbery to all aspects of school life that failed to include me. I still have the cherished clipping from the Boston paper which wrote up our graduation exercises. It reports that Mrs. Peabody, who handed out the prizes, had to summon me so often to the dais that she seemed to be singing a refrain called "Auchincloss." Yes, I had come a long way from the darkness of first-form year! Crossing the green June campus in a red blazer with my prize books tucked proudly under my arm, I was indeed pleased with myself.

A WRITER'S CAPITAL

As if my smugness were not enough, I had to add to it a quality peculiarly unlovable in a seventeen-year-old: a tight political and social conservatism. I was like a British magnate who has risen from the ranks of labor to become a peer; I had had to work too hard to get where I was to care to denigrate the glory of the Groton establishment. I swallowed, in one great convulsive gulp, the rector and his whole system — or what I conceived to be his system. In actual fact, he was far more liberal than I. But I presumed to look behind him, as I had presumed to look behind my parents, to the capitalistic bastions of his and their world. With what I primly decided was a greater honesty than either he or they had risen to, I accepted that bastion as I accepted that world. In 1936, in New Haven, the next time I saw FDR's cortege, then on campaign, I waved a Landon sunflower before the presidential Packard and was slapped in the face by a policeman. I had it coming to me.

MALCOLM STRACHAN

My GROTON ACADEMIC CURRICULUM, with the substantial exceptions of mathematics and history (the latter limited to the United States and Europe), was dominated by languages: Latin, Greek, French, English. As in many schools of the time, copying the English public school theory, Latin was king. I still think that there might have been some sense in this had we learned Latin. There was no reason under the sun why intelligent boys, with as much time as we had to put in, should not have learned to read Latin as fluently as French, and then the world of the ancients would have been opened to us and a whole new dimension of history and thought supplied. But this goal was sacrificed to the narrow one of scrupulously accurate translations. Even as sixth formers we would be asked to render a Latin sentence first into "choctaw," a word-by-word literal translation showing that we had comprehended the use of every tense and case. After that we would put the passage into "beautiful English." As an exercise it was fine, but my point is that we never progressed much beyond the exercise. If we were set down in Julius Caesar's Rome today, I doubt that one of us would be able to get his toga pressed.

In Greek we did have a master, Bill Cushing, who kept this goal of quick reading in mind, and he pitched us into Homer headfirst. But here the trouble, at least for me, was just the reverse. The time allotted to Greek was but a fraction of that given to Latin — one could not even elect it until fourth-form year — and Mr. Cushing hurried over the grammar so fast that I never got my feet on any lingual terra firma. Consequently, my brief romp into the *Iliad* and Euripides has left hardly a trace.

In French, a faint but definite beginning was made in what proved a lifelong taste: seventeenth-century drama — Molière, Racine, Corneille. But it was with Louis Zahner and the Victorian novel that I had my first passionate literary experience. Zahner was not a sentimental man. He belonged more to the eighteenth than to the nineteenth century: he preferred *Tom Jones* and *Peregrine Pickle* to *Pendennis* and *Lorna Doone*. But he was also very wise and kind, qualities essential to a great teacher, and he knew that the fragile bud of literary interest had to be watered no matter what shape it initially took. The fact that I proved a Victorian of Victorians in no way distressed him. One had to make a start. He encouraged me in my enthusiasm for the Brontës, even for Anne, and for the most saccharine sections of Dickens. I reveled in the melancholy atmosphere of these novels, the moors in *Wuthering Heights* and the marshes in *Great Expectations*. I preferred to read them in nineteenth-century editions with black and white illustrations of sad women in dark dresses with long hair. It was the time also when I discovered the *Rubáiyát* and recited the quatrains to myself on autumnal afternoons as I strolled to the Nashua River with a fine feeling of futility.

But there was another side to my reading. Like my compositions, it was sullied by the compulsion to obtain high grades. Instead of giving myself the luxury of reading at will, I marshaled the Victorian novelists into a little army whose function it was to raise my monthly average. I never allowed a minute of valuable reading time to be wasted on a detective story, on a tale of adventure, or even on a classic in a field unrelated to my English course. It was true that I enjoyed much of my reading, but my enjoyment was always incidental to my goal.

At just this period of my worst grubbing after marks a new teacher of English arrived at Groton. Malcolm Strachan had been raised in Brooklyn, but he had spent five years after the age of eighteen in Cambridge, England, where with the extraordinary power of osmosis that always characterized him he seemed to have extracted all that was finest in British culture while rejecting its Philistine coating. He was a man of gentle and charming personality with the absolute courage of a Christian martyr under a seemingly pliable surface. He was sensitive and intense, with the perfect manners that so often attend total honesty and kindness, and he soon won the respect and affection of the boys, who were quick to recognize that a nature devoid of hypocrisy and cant was not necessarily a weak one. Because I had the good fortune to be in his dormitory during his first year, we became friends early. I was able, so to speak, to buy Strachan stock before everyone had learned its value.

Malcolm cared nothing for marks, nothing for worldly distinctions. To break through our schoolboy preconceptions he would hand out to his class mimeographed copies of poems, without date or name of author, and invite an open discussion of them. One did not know if one were reading the verse of Tennyson or that of Ella Wheeler Wilcox. At first I felt vaguely outraged by what seemed to me a rather Bolshevik procedure, but in time I began to be intrigued by the new sense of being alone with a poem, free of other judgments or prejudices, and free, above all, of "marks."

Malcolm as a teacher operated like Thackeray as a novelist.

Thackeray moves slowly around his central subject, Becky
Sharp or Colonel Newcome, a bit like a guide in a museum,
chatting with us, taking us into his confidence, telling us little-
known facts about great events, showing us all his cards, even
admitting that he is a novelist making up his story. Yet at all
times the particular object is kept before our eyes, and at last
some intimation of its beauty and meaning begins to be borne
in upon us, almost without specific description. Malcolm could
approach a play or a poem from any scene or line, or from an
anecdote about the author, or an adverse criticism. All doors,
after all, led into the temple. But as we began to approach any
central meaning, his words, usually so vividly chosen and em-
phasized, would begin to stutter into something like incoher-
ence, and he would clench his fists and seem to be almost in
pain. But this very loss of articulation, of anything remotely
like glibness, made us feel some of the depth of the work and
the rewards that might attend its successful plumbing.

I close my eyes and see Malcolm discussing *Macbeth*. He
would be brilliant and very funny about the trivial questions
one put to him: had Lady Macbeth been married before; had
she had children; who was the third assassin of Banquo; was
MacDuff to be blamed for leaving his family behind? But as
we moved on into the dark tragedy, he would become more
somber, and in the climactic scene in which Duncan's heir
tests MacDuff, where in the daylight of an ordered English
world we look suddenly back to the dark nightmare of Scotland, he would quote in grave, mournful tones the lines in
which the prince describes his own imagined vices that are
really, of course, those of the tyrant:

> Nay, had I power, I should
> Pour the sweet milk of concord into Hell,
> Uproar the universal peace, confound
> All unity on Earth.

And I would whisper silently, "O, Scotland! Scotland!" with MacDuff. Hitler was beginning to be in the headlines; I felt emotionally prepared for him.

Teaching *King Lear*, Malcolm would concentrate carefully, even meticulously, on the language of the King and of Edmund in the first act, contrasting the artificial self-dramatization and irresponsibility of the old man's wishing to retain "the name and all the addition of a king" while crawling unburdened toward death, with the "naturalness" of the bastard son of Gloucester. But by the time we had reached the climax of the heath scene, he would be so awed by the titanic drama unleashed that we would resort to reading the play aloud. I remember his choosing to read Edgar's arcane gibberish as poor Tom. It seemed, if this be not to stretch things absurdly, his chance to express his own humility before the giant sweep of the tragedy.

Gerard Manley Hopkins was a favorite poet of Malcolm's, and I think he must have gone through an agony of soul-wrestling not too dissimilar from that described by Hopkins in "Carrion Comfort" before deciding, in his late thirties, to become an Episcopal priest. Malcolm associated this poem, quite logically, with another favorite of his: Keats's "Ode on Melancholy," and when one heard him read the two aloud, one suspected that they echoed some deep inner temptation of his own:

> No, no, go not to Lethe, neither twist
>   Wolf's-bane, tight-rooted, for its poisonous wine;
> Nor suffer thy pale forehead to be kissed
>   By nightshade, ruby grape of Proserpine . . .

and

> Not, I'll not, carrion comfort, Despair, not feast on thee;
> Not untwist — slack they may be — these last strands of man
> In me or, most weary, cry *I can no more. I can.* . . .

When Malcolm read the first line of the great sestet of "Carrion Comfort," "Why? That my chaff might fly; my

grain lie, sheer and clear," his emphasis of the two final adjectives gave me a feeling of the balm and peace that he desperately needed and desperately sought. Yet nobody, at the same
time, could be more amused by funny books. He would shout
with laughter over Mr. Collins and Lady Catherine de Bourgh.
And certainly nobody more enjoyed the roll of pompous, de-
clamatory verse. I can still hear him reading Marlowe's *Tambur-
laine* with John Alsop, Joe and Stewart's younger brother. One
felt that the two of them were riding together in triumph
through Persepolis.

My point has been labored. Malcolm *lived* in literature
when he read it. Never have I met a person who more perfectly proved the point that every piece of writing is essentially a partnership between author and reader — and an equal
partnership at that. Because the perfect reader is harder to find
than the perfect author, there is a wide tendency to discredit
the role of the former, or to confuse it with that of critic. The
critic is something else altogether. Malcolm was not a critic.
So far as I know, he never published anything. But it always
seemed to me that he had reached a state of communication
with the writer that was beyond articulation, or one that made
articulation seem unneeded. Most, perhaps all, critics tend to
be thinking as they read: "What am I going to say about this?"
It may be a small mote in the eye, but it is still a mote. Malcolm had no such defect, which helped him to be a great
teacher of boys, for he was able to convey a basic enthusiasm
which was worth a hundred ideas.

Malcolm perfectly understood that reading with me had
been almost lost as a pleasure. He saw that it had been chan-
neled, along with everything else in my life, into the muddy
stream of mere distinction seeking. But he was never so clumsy
as to say so. He simply took pains to show me alternatives. He
did not really succeed, at least while I was at Groton, for I

was too fixed in my obsession. But he presented the model of a different life, and I was not so benighted that I failed to perceive the high quality of it. I was wise enough to attach myself to him as closely as one could to a master. He came to visit my family in vacations, and I was pleased and proud when I found how quickly my mother appreciated him, but ultimately jealous when she monopolized him. People were always having this experience with Malcolm. They would think, because he was shy and unpushing, that they might have him all to themselves. Actually, he shone like a diamond in a junk pile. Everyone wanted him.

Malcolm's close relationship with the rector, which provided the source of inspiration for my novel, *The Rector of Justin*, developed after I graduated from Groton. While I was still at school, Malcolm was too young and new; Peabody too old and formidable. But the rector cared more for faith than for anything else, and the younger man's passionate interest in the ministry ultimately drew them together. After Malcolm had been ordained and had returned to Groton as an assistant chaplain as well as a faculty member, he became the spiritual intimate of Peabody's last years. I suspect that the rector found much relief and comfort in this friendship with a devoted disciple who still did not treat him as a legend. He was able to tell Malcolm things that he could tell nobody else: things about his disappointments, for example. Nobody else could believe that he had any. Nobody else could believe that his had not been the happiest and most successful of lives. But the rector, although a great headmaster, was basically a humble man. He knew in his heart that half the Groton family paid only lip service to his ideals. He knew that Mammon dominated his graduates and that he had failed to persuade his boys to receive Christ. Yet he was so surrounded by what I can only call a conspiracy of applause — applause by men who wanted him to believe that he had succeeded because, believing in nothing themselves but their own boyhood faith in him, they could not face a world which had disillusioned the rector — that the facts were hard to come by. Malcolm's love and compassion made the frame for a clear window into truth.

On his side, Malcolm's position was of the simplest. He loved the rector and, quite seriously, regarded him as a saint. The only times that I ever heard him speak with grating harshness about other human beings were when he spoke of persons who had hurt the rector. When Peabody died, very suddenly at the wheel of his car which he had just parked by the side of the road, Malcolm bought the automobile from the estate and preserved it almost as a relic. He and I over the years used to discuss a novel that he was vaguely planning to write about the rector or about a headmaster like the rector, and his school and his theology. He believed that the rector's theology was subtler and more complicated than any of us supposed. But Malcolm's genius was not for writing, and long before his premature death of heart trouble, he had abandoned any such idea. I told him that I would do the book myself and ultimately I did — or my idea of it.

My first plan was that the novel should be cast in the form of the diary of a young master writing the life of a headmaster he believes to be a saint. The Jamesian tour de force would be that the reader should gradually divine that the saint is not the headmaster but the diarist. But I found the idea too difficult to work out. I had no knowledge of saints and really very little interest in them. What was basic to my book (as it never would have been to Malcolm's) was the relationship between the two men. What I saw clearly was that it could be most effectively dramatized if they were opposites in every respect — except in their faith. This faith would be their common denominator, and it would be unique, too, on the school campus. It would be a solitary lantern on a dark plain of worldly things, but it would still be strong enough to confer a distinction which the plain would never have enjoyed without it.

When, as I indicated earlier, I finally decided upon Judge Hand as the partial model for my headmaster, Francis Prescott, I had to bring the younger master into being in terms of his opposites. He had to be shy and timid where Prescott was bullying and rough; he had to be fumbling and inarticulate where Prescott was savagely clear; he had to be naive where Prescott was worldly-wise; and so forth. That is how the character of Brian Aspinwall arose. My process resulted in a much weaker and less attractive man than Malcolm had ever been, and this caused some misunderstandings among his friends who recognized the relationship and assumed that I was trying to draw both Malcolm and the rector to the life. But such are the risks of the novelist's trade. I am still sure in my heart that Malcolm would have approved. I am sure also that he would not have accused me of writing that book "for marks."

TRAVEL AND FANTASY

THE ONLY TIME that we traveled as a family before I was six-
teen was in the summer of 1930, after my first-form year at
Groton, when we made a brief and unsuccessful visit to a dude
ranch in Wyoming. Mother, away from her home base, had
no defenses against her anxieties. She was always an impossible
traveler. We were allowed only the shortest rides on the sleepi-
est horses, and we never once took a pack trip, which in the
eyes of most children was the whole point of going to a ranch.
It was a relief to everybody when we came back to Long Island, and there were no further compromises between my family and the "wilderness" except when my sister, who had
missed the western trip, was permitted to spend a night out
in the woods in Bar Harbor accompanied by her governess and
an immense pile of bedding that was dragged over the pine
needles by the reluctant chauffeur.

If my eyes no longer turned west, they turned resolutely
enough east, and I began to feel deprived, as I passed my fifteenth and sixteenth birthdays, because I had never been to
Europe. Many of my form at Groton had been, and I sus-

pected that they were my cultural superiors by the mere fact of having breathed that richer air. Mother had breathed it, and at a much earlier age than mine, and I pored enviously through her scrapbooks which showed her mother and aunts (the Dixons clung together even in travel) in long dresses and big hats before Fontainebleau or the Tower of London. Mother had even watched the coronation procession of Edward VII from a balcony, and Father, as a Yale undergraduate, had visited an aunt, married to a count, in a fabulous Swedish castle. And what had they done for me?

At last, in response to persistent begging, it was resolved that we should take a family trip to England and France, and in June of 1934 we sailed on the *Champlain* for Southampton. My excitement was so great that I was not even too much mortified when Mother sent a note up to the captain in a heavy mist to suggest that he blow the foghorn more frequently. I was even a bit thrilled by the Corneille sentiment expressed in the card that he courteously sent back from the bridge: "Madame, la Marine Française ne connâit pas le brouillard." But Mother had little use for the French concept of "gloire," and in later summers she was to show a preference for German vessels.

We were up early to catch the first glimpse of the coast of Ireland. Even traveling today, whenever the wheels of a plane touch European soil, I can recapture some of that early excitement. It has never been at all the same kind of thrill for me to arrive anywhere in this hemisphere, or in the Pacific, or in Asia. The thrill is associated exclusively with "Europe." There were to be long dull months in small dull ports in England and France during World War II when I would almost be able to shake off my ennui by reminding myself what continent I was on. It gave me reassurance when I discovered that Henry James, after a lifetime of living in Europe, had never entirely got over the same feeling.

It may have been my exuberance that caused me, that first night in Fleming's Hotel in London, to overflow my bath. Unhappily, there was a drought, and the evening papers had announced that even His Majesty was using only two inches in his tub. The wanton cascade, which seemed an insult to George V himself, penetrated the floor and inundated the reception desk below. Shrinking into the back of the elevator the next morning I heard the members of a county family, who had come up to Fleming's for the season, holding forth in disgust about the iniquity of "that American boy."

But nothing could stem the excitement of seeing London, not even the scorn of my fellow lodgers, not even the deplorable way Mother behaved in restaurants, seeing disease and contamination in every glass and dish. My only disappointments sprang from the fact that, approaching everything historically, I was totally unprepared for the ravages of time. When I wanted to see palaces such as Whitehall or Nonesuch, or later in Paris the Tuileries or St. Cloud, it was a shock to discover that they had not existed for dozens or even hundreds of years. Father was heard to remark: "The Europe Louis came to see no longer exists!" Only in the Place de la Bastille was I prepared to find a void. But even voids were exciting in "Europe."

Europe that summer and the next, in England, France, Italy, and Greece, unrolled for me like a library. Versailles was Saint-Simon; London, Dickens; Warwickshire, Shakespeare. In the theater at Epidaurus I tested the acoustics by reciting in Greek the dozen lines I knew of Homer to my brother John sitting in the top row in back. In Paris I made my poor parents sit through three hours of *Le Monde où l'on s'ennuie* preceded by a curtain raiser, Musset's *Caprice*, which ran for an hour. My travels might have been compiled into a "Reader's Companion to European Literature" with the persistent footnotes of Mother's desperate worrying. I still see her on the Moher

The Auchincloss summer home in Newport about 1865

Father at fifty-three

Mother, as she appeared to me at six

Bovee School about 1927 (the second house from the left)

With my older brother and sister, 1921

"The Bray," at Lawrence, Long Island, 1926

In Wyoming with Mother, 1930

"Schooner Head," Bar Harbor, Maine

Locust Valley, Long Island —
the only home my parents ever built

Endicott Peabody as painted
by Ellen Emmet Rand

The chapel of Groton School

At Groton, 1934

Malcolm Strachan in 1941   Writing a novel, summer 1940

Jack Woods (right) in 1941, a few hours before his death

On board the USS *Moonstone*, 1943

Amélie Rives at fifty

Ruth Draper

Aileen Tone with Henry
Adams in 1914

Aileen Tone in her
eighties

Cliffs in Ireland pleading with us, though a hundred yards from the edge, to get down on our hands and knees!

To explain why these trips were such strong stimulants to my imagination, I should emphasize the monopoly which Europe then enjoyed on all the intellectual outlets of American East Coast youth. We were living well before the explosion of interest in domestic art, literature, or history. Neither at Bovee nor at Groton had I been exposed to more than a trickle of the work of American writers. United States history was taught, it was true, and taught quite thoroughly, but it was generally considered a bore. There were no kings or queens, no popes or cardinals, no poisons or tortures, no sex — only a good deal of windy oratory from elderly political men. I am not saying that there were not exciting tales of red Indians, or that I did not enjoy *The Scarlet Letter*, but essentially drama and romance lay to the east, across the Atlantic. There the books I cared about were illustrated before my eyes.

The extent to which literature has remained associated in my mind with transatlantic travel can be shown by an absurd example. A few years ago, flying into Paris, as the plane passed over Brittany I pointed out a famous monument to my neighbor. He was understandably confused when I exclaimed: "See, it's over there! That spire. *Mont-Saint-Michel and Chartres!*"

Aesthetic impulses now began to press upon me, at home as well as abroad. There was even a period toward the end of my Groton career when I visualized myself as a future actor. If I turned to adults for inspiration, they were now apt to be persons with philosophies very much at variance from my mother's. The elderly wife of a senior master at Groton, a true *précieuse*, was the author of a slender volume of poetry which, years earlier in a fit of nerves, she had snatched away from the press, just before publication. In the rarefied atmosphere of her Elizabethan parlor she and I read these poems aloud. I felt in communication with a kindred soul.

But the superaesthete in my life was "Aunt Marie." She was not really an aunt but one of those lovable old maids known as such to the children of their friends. She was an acutely intelligent if rather whimsical soul, with a heavy-handed sentimentality but an eye for art and an ear for music. She dressed in a mannish way and was a great preserver of relics and mementos. Well-to-do herself and befriended by the rich, she was always provided with boxes for concerts and operas, and her hospitality was unbounded. What fascinated me was her unabashed philosophy of art for art's sake. Aunt Marie lived for beauty: in a rose, in a symphony, in a slant of morning light, in an ode, in the East River, in Wagner, above all in Wagner. In the old Metropolitan Opera House she wanted to have his name inscribed in the scalloped shield directly over the center of the stage. She had heard more than fifty performances of *Tristan* there. Yet she had no sense of rustic beauty. Hers was a totally urban soul. She used to tell us, when we left town for the weekend: "If you see a tree, give it a kick for me."

I was early aware of my parents' antagonism to Aunt Marie's principles, and I plunked right down on her side. It was not only the desire to irritate Mother; it was also that I suspected that Aunt Marie's rather groggy delight in the "Liebestod" represented something more wonderful than anything my parents had, or at least something that I might myself attain if I should fail to attain whatever it was that my parents had. Perhaps I should find that I really belonged to Aunt Marie's world. Perhaps it would provide the ultimate escape from Father's downtown. But there were troubling factors here. First, Aunt Marie's artistic indulgences depended on downtown money, a point that Father never failed to stress. Secondly, Mother's criticism of Aunt Marie's sentimentality and "gushiness," of her habit of beating time heavily to music, of her easy tears and faraway look, was only too painfully valid. I was too sensible myself to go all the way with Aunt Marie's theories.

In the end Aunt Marie let me down. She threw away the battle for beauty by taking to drink. I was bitter about it; much as I loved her, I could not forgive her for proving Mother right. What a warning to the would-be aesthete! When I had to spend the intermission at the opera sneaking old-fashioneds from the bar into Aunt Marie's box, I would reflect grimly on the fate of those who forsook the rules of moderation and reason to gambol in the halls of beauty. Poor Aunt Marie! She was like Blanche DuBois in *A Streetcar Named Desire*. For all her imagined glimpses of a finer world, she was betrayed into the clutches of the Philistines by a vice which excited their ridicule and cast a dirty doubt on all her aspirations.

In my last year at Groton I was convinced that simply to live in Europe might be a justifiable existence, and when a form mate told me that his family was considering sending him to the University of Grenoble, I regarded him as the happiest of youths. It would not have occurred to me to ask my parents for such a privilege, but when, on a weekend visit at just this time, Father told me that I did not have to go to Yale simply because he had done so, that, on the contrary, I could choose my own college, I seized the unbelievable chance.

"Then I'll go to Grenoble!" I cried.

Father was caught quite off guard, but after a moment he recovered and qualified his offer.

"I meant any college in the United States. I think you need a lot more, rather than a lot less, of America."

So I chose Yale.

YALE

IN THE EARLY 1950s there were a series of famous trials in the Federal District Court for the Southern District of New York involving the issue of Communist espionage. We had the two Alger Hiss trials, the trial of William Remington and those of the Communist party leaders. At the risk of appearing like a Roman fan of gladiatorial contests, I must admit that I found these cases absorbingly interesting. I was then a law clerk in Sullivan & Cromwell, and my duties took me frequently to the Surrogate's Court. I would step across Foley Square to watch one of the trials "just for a minute" and then stay for hours. It was a wonder how I ever got my work done.

My sympathies in the Remington case were all with the defendant. He was an exact contemporary. He had been at Dartmouth while I was at Yale. He was tall and handsome, and he made an appealing witness. Presumably to establish his early membership in the party, which he had denied, Remington's letters to his family from college were read aloud by the prosecution. They were full of references to labor conditions and strikes. It was just while I was considering, with a twinge of conscience, how different they were from my own letters from Yale, full of nonsense about parties and theaters, that the man sitting next to me leaned over to whisper:

"You can see the rot starting way back then."

I was shocked. Was *that* the difference between Remington and me? Was that earnest and passionate young man, who had wanted to tell his family all the things that obsessed him about social injustice, rotten? And was I, the dilettante, absorbed in my own petty social and intellectual pursuits, the preferable type of undergraduate? Oh, no, everything in my conscience had to reject the idea then as it rejects it now. Remington might have taken a wrong path, but surely the heart and sensitivity with which he had started were good. When he was later murdered in prison, I saw an obscenity in the blue sky of my old-fashioned Yankee idealism.

I went to Yale in the fall of 1935. My older brother, then a second-year law student, drove me to New Haven, and that same night we went to the movies and saw *The Thirty-Nine Steps*. How unlike Groton! I had a sense of heady liberation. John and I had been all over the Mediterranean that summer together, which might have seemed liberation enough, but that was different. That was vacation. Here we were in an institution of learning, a school no less, and what were we doing? Going to the movies! And what was more, we could go to the movies the next night, every night, if we were silly enough to choose to. The strict boarding school of those days at least had the advantage of providing ecstasy to its new graduates. Groton was like the salt that Keats is supposed to have rubbed on his tongue to intensify the delights of wine.

And truly Yale, in the three years I remained there, did provide an enchanted interlude. More than any other period of my youth it was a hedonistic time, in which I cultivated freely the pleasures that appealed to me. These were not the pleasures that appealed to most young men, but my very freedom from their standards constituted an added delight. I went to only two football games in my whole New Haven career, and I steered clear of campus activities except to write four little stories for the *Yale Literary Magazine* and to play two small roles in Dramatic Society productions. Not surprisingly, I received no bid to join a fraternity. But I was perfectly happy with my courses, my little clique of new friends, and the easy availability of New York with its parties and theaters.

Conscience, however, had not entirely deserted me. I elected a course in physics because I thought I "ought to," and it almost cost me my Phi Beta Kappa key. I had not lost sight of the gray world of adulthood where men had to sell or manufacture things, or advise sellers and manufacturers how to keep within the law. When I thought of law school, I still shuddered. My brother John, it seemed to me, suffered under deadly courses, and I glanced away uneasily from the heavy casebooks on his desk. All that would come in time. But in the meanwhile I was granted this odd reprieve between the long effort of Groton and the long effort of life, and I might as well make the most of it.

I could delight in Chauncey Tinker, that glorious old ham, weeping over the death of Keats. I could revel in John Allison posturing on the dais as Saint Bernard preaching a crusade at Vézelay. I could drive out to Farmington and visit my enviable cousin Wilmarth Lewis encased in the glories of his Horace Walpole collection. I could see Nazimova in *Ghosts*, John Gielgud in *Hamlet*. I could hear Flagstad as Isolde and Brunhilde. I could read Shakespeare aloud at Professor Samuel Hemingway's; I could talk bad French over a vermouth cassis at a causerie at Jonathan Edwards College. And I could drink deep on Saturday nights with friends who did not seem to understand that life had to be grim. Perhaps it didn't, for them. Perhaps they were exempt.

For a young man who was shy with girls I went to an extraordinary number of debutante parties. But my interest was in the spectacle. I "collected" parties. I would go to one where I knew nobody at all, simply because it was given in a house or a club that I wanted to see or because something interested me about my host or hostess. I was fascinated by New York families and loved to push back into the past for the origin of each. I became something of a joke for my cultivation of the ancient, and I remember being seated, at a dinner before the Tuxedo Ball, at a tiny table with old Mrs. Tilford, its founder. And at a coming-out party at the Breakers in Newport, I spent a large part of my evening talking to an elderly man who recalled a dance given in that same hall by the Vanderbilts at the turn of the century when footmen in maroon livery had lined the whole of the great marble stairway. What different things Bill Remington must have been studying!

I have often noted that a favorite topic of novelists of manners is the disillusionment of the young hero from the outlying provinces, geographical or social, who enters the "great world." At first it dazzles him. It is all dukes and duchesses, glittering jewels and decorations, sparkling lights and sparkling talk. Once initiated, however, he soon discovers that it is banal, stale, and malicious. Proust, of course, is the supreme example of this. But if there is to be disillusionment there has to have been illusion, and how many clever young men (for these heroes are always clever) suffer from the illusion that the "great world" is brilliant? Proust himself knew all about the Faubourg Saint-Germain before he ever entered it. I suspect that the hero's illusion about society is a device which permits his creator to describe his own fascination with it without seeming a snob. What attracted Proust to the Faubourg was not its wit but its titles. Social climbers are apt to invent virtues for the worlds which they seek to join. But I can say truly that I was never "disillusioned" by society. I was perfectly clear from the beginning that I was interested in the story of money: how it was made, inherited, lost, spent. It never occurred to me that society people would be any more interesting than other people or that I would hear unusually stimulating talk at dinner parties. That was not what I went for.

Mother saw my social life exactly as I saw it, an interlude, but she saw it as a rather dangerous one. Would I ever get back to the business of serious living? She and I had already at this point established the deep congeniality that was to last to the end, a mutual sympathy and compatibility that made communication a wonderfully simple affair. We noticed the same things and laughed at the same things. We had similar habits of mind and the same ways of leaping to conclusions, the same lazinesses. But there was always, alas, the division caused by her nagging sense of a responsibility to turn me into a man like the other men in her world, or at least into a reasonable facsimile thereof, and my own angry resentment of her refusal to see that I might be something altogether different: a great writer, a great actor, a great professor, a great individualist, a great *something*. She was determined that I was only a dilettante, and she was clear that dilettantism had to be kept under rigid control. Otherwise one ended up making an ass of oneself playing butlers' parts in Broadway comedies or writing *vers de société* or *romans à clef* that only one's friends bought and snickered at. And to make an ass of oneself before the world, our world, Mother's world anyway, was the worst kind of hubris a man could commit and was apt to bring down on his offending head a well-merited thunderbolt.

Of course, deep down, I agreed with her. That was why my resentment went so deep. She, fortunate female, could afford to be a dilettante for her whole life. She could sit home all day if she chose, and read book after book. She could spend her nights at theaters and at dinner parties (not that she wanted to) and people would only cry: "Isn't Priscilla wonderful?

Isn't your mother wonderful?" And what sympathy did she have for me, a poor male fated to drown in the dark dull sea of American male life? Sympathy? Was she not tearing what she considered the defective life belt out of my arms? Why, I wondered angrily, could I not have had one of those vapid, lisping, ever-blonde mothers who would have said: "Darling, I just know you're going to write the great American novel!" I wouldn't have believed her, but it would have soothed me.

Far from soothing, Mother thought it was her duty to be constantly warning her children not to idealize, not to romanticize life. She seemed to believe that there was some moral fault in the process of being disappointed, perhaps because it showed that one had too much presumed — hubris again. She loved to quote Frances Cornford's quatrain:

> A young Apollo, golden-haired,
> Stands dreaming on the verge of strife,
> Magnificently unprepared
> For the long littleness of life.

Mother deplored my courses at Yale because they were not "practical." I remember her asking me at a Sunday lunch party what I was writing my history term paper about and then turning to her guests to exclaim: "The Medici popes! Here is the world going to pieces before our very eyes, and Louis is deep in the Medici popes." No doubt she would have been happier had I come home, like Bill Remington, with a long list of labor grievances. They would have bored her, but Mother never minded being bored by what she considered a worthy interest.

From the perspective of today, it seems to me that my courses at Yale were thoroughly practical. For they have stayed by me for a lifetime, and what could be more practical than that? I suppose it could be argued that the same taste which induced me to elect Joseph Seronde's courses in French drama and fiction, Chauncey Tinker's in English poetry, and Samuel

Hemingway's in Shakespeare would have led me in any event to the literature which they taught. It is quite possible. But how often do we see that happen to people in the workaday world? It seems to me that the tragedy of not using the college years to learn the best in art and literature, at least for those of artistic or literary inclination, is that never again does one receive impressions with quite the same kind of emotional intensity with which one receives them between the ages of seventeen and twenty-one. It is so brief a time, so very brief, yet one can build a lifetime on the exploitation of it. Surely this is proved by the American habit of reunions. Why should so many thousands of middle-aged and old men and women go back annually to their alma maters if it were not for the memory of a time of intenser feeling? Why should they give so many millions of dollars to college endowment funds? Would they do as much for any institution that happened to represent any other four years of their lives?

FIRST NOVEL

My CLOSEST FRIEND at Yale and the person who had the greatest influence on me in this period of my life was Jack Woods, my roommate of sophomore and junior years. Jack was a brilliant, nervous youth, plain of feature and awkward of build, but with lively, laughing, penetrating eyes. He had an insight into other people's thoughts and motives that was uncanny and at times disturbing. He was quick, entertaining, affectionate, suspicious. He came from Orange, New Jersey, the only child of a broken home, with small, but just adequate, means. His father, brilliant and erratic like Jack, had committed suicide during our sophomore year. Jack was intensely emotional, greedy for every kind of experience in life and grimly determined to make up for his own native deficiencies in looks, in love, in social distinction. He could be very kind, and his sensitivity helped him here, but it also helped him on occasion to be cruel. His character had no axis, his heart no serenity, and he killed himself in 1941, while a reporter on the *Herald Tribune*. The astonishment was general. Everyone had assumed he was on the threshold of a great career.

In his resolution to get everything he could out of life, Jack
was still discriminating. Success and power might be the reali-
ties of post-college life, but they could await that life. Success
on the campus was something else. Jack took a hard look
through this success to see what was really behind it. He decided at length, despite all the outward seriousness of youth
at Yale, that the ultimate reality behind the hurly-burly of
undergraduate competition was a simple pursuit of pleasure.
Fun was what Yale was basically all about. It behooved Jack
Woods, therefore, to have more fun than anyone else. There
was, in this respect, something rather quaintly old-fashioned
about him, a hangover of the jazz era into the soberer thirties,
a touch of Scott Fitzgerald (whom he much admired) in a character as naturally somber as the more contemporary Thomas
Wolfe.

Jack saw in me a key to a social world that was not readily
available to him. He was on none of the lists of eligible young
men provided by entertainment bureaus for the mothers of
debutantes, but it was easy enough for anyone on such a list
to bring his college roommate to a party. I took Jack to many
of these, though not so many as he wanted. But after a while
he no longer needed me; he found he could splash happily
alone in those mild waters. His wit and his acumen more than
compensated for an unprepossessing appearance and a small
bank balance. The reason I did not more resent being used as
a footstool (a ladder would imply too great a height to be
scaled) was that Jack disarmed me with his total frankness.
And then, too, he was the best company in the world. Even
when I was most afraid of his probing insight and mordant
judgments, I had still to admire the accuracy of his divinations.

Jack and I became editors together of the *Yale Lit.* As I recall, he gained his editorship on the basis of a single story. He
loved to talk about his writing, though he wrote very little. He
professed to emulate Henry James, to whose novels he intro-

76

duced me and in whose subtleties Jack's subtle nature took infinite and sometimes perverse delight. But the great thing that he did for me was to shake (at least temporarily) my inhibition about becoming a professional writer.

I should first explain this inhibition, of which the reader will have already sensed the source in my mother's philosophy. I believed (deep down in my bowels, if not in my intellect) that a man born to the responsibilities of a brownstone bourgeois world could only be an artist or writer if he were a genius, that he should not kick over the traces unless a resounding artistic success, universally recognized, should justify his otherwise ridiculous deviation. The world might need second-class lawyers and doctors; it did not need a second-class artist. This belief was premised, not so much on the ignorance of arts and letters in the upper-middle-class world of Manhattan, as in the tradition of such an ignorance, a tradition in which Mother had largely grown up and which must have flourished in "Dixon Alley." Mother always tended to justify the Philistinism in her family which she saw as a healthy judgment on her own deviant intellectualism.

But Jack Woods had a more normal point of view. He did not live in the New York of my mother's limited vision. He saw the city more as the site of Broadway than of Wall Street. To him a playwright or novelist was fully the peer of a lawyer or stockbroker. When I asked him how the young, unrecognized writer was to live, he would simply say "teach," anticipating the great haven that academe has since become for creative artists. Nor did a literary career in Jack's opinion necessarily foreclose others. A writer could go into politics; a writer could be a businessman. I began, timidly at first, to visualize a new future. I saw myself teaching English at Yale. The fantasy rapidly grew. I pictured myself on a dais before two hundred students rapt in silence as I described the death of Shelley. I saw the intellectually curious coming to my study afterwards to ask questions about my latest novel. What heaven!

But could I write a novel? I had my *Madame Bovary* already conceived. All I had to do now was put it on paper. To ensure some degree of quiet and to avoid prying eyes (particularly Jack's), I made a habit of spending my afternoons in the Linonia Brothers Reading Room in the Sterling Library, and there I wrote the story of Audrey Emerson, a schoolteacher who married her way into society. The words tumbled out of me, and I was happy as I had never been happy before. But then I had never really written before. My stories, at school and at Yale, had been exercises. This tale of Audrey was part of me. I learned then and there that all a novelist's characters are himself. There may be a character who is the author dressed up to look like John Jones or Mary Smith, but it is still basically the author.

My novel was intended to be a determinist novel. Given my heroine, with her assets and liabilities, given her background and family, given her likely chances and likely temptations, then the plot of the book had logically to follow. My idea was to endow Audrey with fifty percent of every quality. She should be half-intellectual, half-ambitious, half-spiritual, half-worldly, half-sensuous, half-frigid, and she should be fixed at the start right in the center of the social ladder. It seemed to me that such a creature would be just attractive enough to be dangerous and just indecisive enough to be destructive.

Looking back over my first plot, I see the sources bristle. After graduating from a small college in New England (Middlebury, Vermont) Audrey gets a job teaching in an exclusive girls' school in New York (Miss Chapin's). Engaged as a tutor to give supplementary home work to a rich girl in her class, Lila Sabatière, Audrey is dazzled by the great house and gracious living of Lila's parents. She attracts Lila's brother, Barclay, a naive and immature Yale student, who, to the horror

78

of his family, proposes to her. Audrey, in a fit of self-disgust at her own mercenary motives, refuses him and marries instead her old college swain, Tommy Littell, whom she thinks she can love because he is so good. Tommy has a job teaching at a boys' boarding school, Chelton (Groton). Audrey finds the faculty wives and their closed society tedious (Emma Bovary). She flirts with Stephen Hill, a rich but neurotic young bachelor, cousin to Lila, who is seeking a precarious happiness by teaching at the school he loved as a boy. Sexually frustrated, he is an easy prey to the bored Audrey. She knows all about his wealth, for he is a nephew of her old employer, Mrs. Sabatière. It is a second, perhaps a last, chance. Her husband discovers the intrigue, divorces her, and Audrey marries Stephen ("Thou hast it all, King, Cawdor, Glamis, all"). She makes a brilliant appearance at Lila Sabatière's coming-out party in Lila and Stephen's grandmother's immense villa in Newport (the Breakers). But Stephen's heart is broken by the fact that he can never return to the beloved school whose headmaster has been scandalized by his conduct. He finds that the woman for whom he has given up his cherished academic life is frivolous and cold. He shoots himself on a weekend at the Sabatières' country place, and it is his silly aunt who finds the body after the neighborhood has searched the woods. Audrey accepts her guilt and refuses her share of her husband's estate. She returns to her alma mater in New England as an instructor. The reader, however dubious, is meant to feel that she is redeemed.

I had my manuscript typed and read it with astonishment. I thought it a masterpiece. I did not show it to Jack because I did not dare. Although he liked me well enough, he was always pulling me to pieces. I knew that plenty of this was envy, but even so it could hurt. Jack had a devilish way of probing the raw nerve. My novel was far too precious a lamb to be exposed to such a wolf.

My parents read it. Mother did not like it at all, but she was very much afraid that somebody might publish it. She anticipated that "the friends" would deplore the vulgarity of the society parts. Father thought it would do me no good if I ever went downtown to work. We agreed that I should submit it to the woman whom Mother considered her most intelligent friend. The latter returned it, asking rather airily if it had any purpose beyond giving the reader a *quart d'heure de plaisir.* My four-hundred-page *Madame Bovary!*

But I would show them all. When it was published, they would regret their obtuseness. I visualized that review on the front page of the Sunday *Times* book review section with its honeyed phrases of "startling new talent" and "an authentic young voice," as thousands of would-be novelists have and continue to imagine it. I packed the novel off to Scribner's and received in a few weeks' time a friendly note rejecting it, but asking to see my "next."

And then my life simply fell to pieces. I was not indignant at Scribner's. I was not even surprised. I actually agreed with their decision now. What caused my acute distress was my sense that the letter was really a message from Jove to warn me that I had been making a fool of myself. What in the name of all that was holy did the likes of me think I was up to, dabbling in literature, rushing around to every play on Broadway, dreaming of teaching, and, worst of all, writing a novel, when all the while I *knew* that my real destiny, my serious destiny, my destiny as a man, was to become a lawyer and submit to the same yoke to which my poor father had so long and patiently submitted?

I decided that something had to be done right away. There had to be an act of expiation followed by a consecration of myself to a "serious" career. I do not say that I articulated this idea in just those terms, but that is how it seems to me now, looking back. I resolved to apply at once to the best law school that would accept me without a degree on the basis of my three years at Yale. Inquiry showed this to be the University of Virginia, and I went down to New York to discuss the matter with my parents.

Father was appalled. He could not understand why I wanted to skip my senior year at Yale. "What's the rush?" he kept not unreasonably asking. "You'll spend the rest of your life explaining why you didn't graduate from Yale." He was right. I have. But Mother understood perfectly. After all, our neuroses were complementary. And I think she approved. I think she was rather relieved to have the idea of my literary career quashed, once and for all. She was very careful and conscientious about using all the arguments for finishing the Yale course, but I distinctly felt that she found my decision a brave and right one. Renunciation appealed to her. She admired those who took without complaining the stiff medicine of their condemnation to routine tasks and dreary rounds. It showed that they were good sports, and to be a good sport about the deities who played fast and loose with one's fate was to show a high style. Father at length consented; he saw that I was determined. The University of Virginia accepted me, and I left Yale.

Perversely enough, in that intervening summer, I wrote half of a second novel. I had gravely pledged to myself that I would not write a word of fiction while at law school, but there seemed no compelling reason not to indulge myself one last time beforehand. My book concerned a foolish, snobbish dilettante called Beverly Stregelinus, a name dreamed up by Jack Woods to be used for a character who would be a caricature of me. Beverly was later to be the hero, or non-hero, of *The Indifferent Children*, my first published novel, where he would pair off with Audrey Emerson, a survivor from the manuscript written at Yale. But in this second abortive work of fiction I traced his shoddy attempts to make a rich marriage which ended, because he was handicapped by sentimentality, in his making one that was neither rich nor happy.

Jack came to visit me in Long Island that summer and asked if he might read the first novel. When I agreed, he read it, almost at a sitting, and then wept. He said that I had derived my idea of Audrey's mercenary nature from his own. I denied this, quite sincerely. Then he accused me of leaving Yale because I disliked him. This too was untrue. But it was true that I was afraid of him. I was afraid that I could not live with the image of myself that I saw reflected in the limpid pool of Jack's mind.

Three years later, in June of 1941, Jack was staying with me in my family's apartment in New York. My parents were in Long Island. He and I had been ushers at a wedding; we had gone to different parties afterwards. When I came home, I found that Jack had been to the apartment but had gone out again. He had left his room in a fearful mess. This was the climax of a series of irritations which had occurred during his visit, so I wrote him a thoroughly nasty note, telling him what a rotten guest he was, and went to bed. The next morning I was awakened by a telephone call to be informed that Jack had fallen to his death from the living room window of a friend's apartment during a late party. He had been drinking heavily, sitting, precariously balanced, on a windowsill.

Under my harsh little note in the hall I found one from Jack. He had come home a second time that night. He had written me of his reasons for not wishing to live any more. He had had the exquisite consideration to understand that I might have worried about the effect of my "silly note." In its clarity, in its courtesy, in its kindness, it was a very wonderful letter. I believe that Jack would have had a remarkable career.

CHARLOTTESVILLE

MR. JEFFERSON'S UNIVERSITY, as it is known in some circles in Virginia, refused from the very beginning to constitute itself an appropriate background for the grim mood in which I had sought it. Driving down to Charlottesville in the fall of 1938 I had stopped in Baltimore, where on that same day Thomas Wolfe had died, and I had been awed by the occurrence of such a tragedy on the very eve of my own nonwriting career. But Charlottesville was not going to play any such ghostly games with me. The white columns and red brick of the "Lawn," the red earth and blue hills of the countryside, compelled me, for the first time in my life, to give a daily consideration to surrounding beauty. I found that in the University of Virginia it was impossible ever to be entirely alone with one's own self-pity. "Mr. Jefferson" was always lurking.

I still consider him the greatest of American architects. It is not an opinion that I can justify with any expertise or that I should care to try to. It may be simply the tug at the heart that I feel before the columns of the Lawn, the serpentine walls, the Rotunda and the arcades, before the dome and façades of

Monticello. It may be in the sense that they convey to me of variety, ingenuity, wit, charm.. The University of Virginia in antebellum days must have been a temple of reason and moderation raising a voice of mild warning to the rampant Yankee mercantilism of the old North and the sullen, surly prejudice of the old South. I have always believed that Virginia fought, not to keep her slaves, but out of a romantic sense of loyalty.

Unlike Yale, the University of Virginia blended with the town and countryside. When I rode, as I did two afternoons a week, I rode with other students or with faculty members or with neighbors who had no connection with the university. Socially, the life was more adult than at Yale. On Saturday nights I was apt to dine out with one or another of the married law students. These were an affluent lot, largely northern, who had rented cottages in the neighborhood of the Farmington Country Club and tended to be cliquey. They were dominated by Marshall Field, Jr., and his wife Joanne, though the Fields reached out to a wider community. Marshall was a dedicated and ambitious law student. He was first in our class and ultimately notes editor of the *Law Review* and president of the Law School. He felt that he had hitherto lived too narrowly and was consciously broadening himself. He wanted to be a part of everything in the university, and he succeeded. Had all his life been modeled on his Charlottesville years, the considerable success which he later enjoyed might have been even greater. Like Marshall, I was exhilarated by our new environment and opened every pore to it.

Most exciting of all was the discovery that I actually liked the study of law. This had not been in the cards at all, and for a while I feared that it might be an illusion. But it persisted. I can remember the precise moment when I realized that it would last. It was in a class in which Hardy Dillard, our contracts professor, discussed a case on implied promises. Dillard was a very interesting lecturer. At times he seemed to be talking to himself, as if lost in the arcane mysteries of a contracts problem. At others he would be silent for quite long periods, as if groping for articulation. But his absorption was somehow contagious. One felt that he was reaching deep into the case to pull out a principle which would go far beyond the mere regulation of current business interests. He was touching, perhaps, on some fundamental of human relations.

The case that struck me as fraught with possibilities other than those which I had hitherto considered merely "legal" was Wood v. Duff-Gordon, decided in 1917 by the Court of Appeals of New York. Judge Cardozo wrote the opinion. The case, as every law student will remember, involved an agreement between a fashion designer, Lady Duff-Gordon, and a salesman, Wood, under the terms of which the salesman was to have the exclusive right to place Lady Duff-Gordon's endorsements on designs, and she was to have half the profits from the sale of such designs. Lady Duff-Gordon, finding the agreement unprofitable, placed her endorsements elsewhere. Her counsel argued that the agreement was not a binding contract because Wood had no obligations under it. Judge Cardozo, deciding in Wood's favor, found that the agreement contained an implied promise on his part to make reasonable efforts to create profits for both partners.

It was not, however, the theory of the case but the language of Judge Cardozo that caught my imagination. His first five sentences established the atmosphere in which the little drama was to unfold:

"The defendant styles herself 'a creator of fashions.' Her favor helps a sale. Manufacturers of dresses, millinery and like articles are glad to pay for a certificate of her approval. The things which she designs, fabrics, parasols and what not, have a new value in the public mind when issued in her name. She employed the plaintiff to help her to turn this vogue into money."

85

I had a picture in my mind of Lady Duff-Gordon. I saw her as attractive, smart, middle-aged, abrupt, careless of the rights of others, using her title and social position to awe small business associates whom she despised. I saw Wood as plain, tough, industrious, unimpressed. I was glad that Justice Cardozo had decided for him. I admired his key sentence: "A promise may be lacking, and yet the whole writing may be instinct with an obligation, imperfectly expressed."

This all sounds silly enough, but the reader must remember that I was reaching for any piece of wood to pitch into the dying fire of my imagination. It was exciting to find a whole log pile. For what was a case but a short story? What was the law but language? Was there any reason that a judge should not be a great writer? Wasn't Cardozo one? Like every author of fiction, he started with a donnée which he then had to dramatize, interpret, make striking and interesting. The individual comedy, or tragedy, had to be fitted into the universal. Whenever I saw the name "Cardozo, J" in one of my case-books I would have a friendly feeling. Here was my leader, my guide, in every field: in contracts, in torts, in taxation, in criminal and constitutional law. I bought his books, *The Nature of the Judicial Process*, *The Growth of the Law*, and, to me of course most important, *Law and Literature*. I read and reread them.

In later years I came to find Cardozo's style a bit labored. I seemed to see him smiling at me behind sentences which had been cut and trimmed like topiary. I learned to prefer the lean, clean prose of Justice Holmes. But the point was that I had found a library of new authors, and that it was a library in which I might perfectly well one day find myself. Nor were the judges the only authors. There were the brief writers, the textbook writers, the great professors. When Noel Dowling took a busman's holiday from Columbia to come down to Charlottesville to teach us constitutional law, I was fascinated by his method of probing to the essence of the political scene by elaborately analyzing the points of view and thought processes, one by one, of the nine Supreme Court justices. Law in Dowling's course became more than literature. It became philosophy, psychology, sociology.

What never quite lost its forbidding quality to me was statute law. Obviously, this was because there were no human beings involved. Not until a statute became involved in a case was my interest kindled. It upset me to see large areas of the common law, hitherto enshrined in the cathedral language of great judges, relegated to obsolescence by the proliferation of codes. Of course, this has now reached a point where the common law hardly exists, and lawyers are more concerned with technical statutes than with majestically written opinions. I do not suggest that this is a bad thing. I merely make the point that if I, a frustrated novelist, had gone to law school today, I doubt that I should have been so quickly consoled for giving up a career of letters.

In the summer after my first year in Charlottesville I completed my novel about Beverly Stregelinus. My interest, however, had been blunted by interim events, and writing out the second half was a discipline. There are some authors who can force their muse. Indeed, there are some whose muse can only be made to work in such a fashion. But that has never been my way, as I was to discover in the only period of my life when I was to dedicate full time to it. Nobody but myself ever read this second novel, but I am convinced that it was without merit. There was a last chapter which dealt with the tacky wedding reception Beverly's show-off but financially bust parents-in-law give to dazzle their undazzled summer colony. Beverly, dancing with the maid of honor who has turned out to be his one true love, discusses, like Sydney Carton in the tumbrel, the beauties of his self-sacrifice. If the sentiment was

Dickensian, the social satire was meant to be Thackerayan. The result was bathos.

I reread the completed manuscript in a morning and decided that only a prompt execution would alleviate my suffering. I removed the penciled pages from the notebooks and placed them neatly in the garbage pail. An hour later I had a twinge of regret and hurried to the back of the house to retrieve my manuscript. Perhaps some of it could be salvaged. But that perfidious bark, the fatal garbage truck, had already made its visit. The pail was empty. It was probably as well. I remembered the death of Wolfe in Baltimore. The heavens themselves seemed to have conspired to show me that I was not to be a writer.

In my last two years in law school I neither read nor wrote any fiction. The *Law Review* absorbed all my literary interests. I used to liken the art of writing what we called a "decision," which was actually a comment on one, to that of writing a sonnet. One summarized the case to be commented on. One gave the origin of the principle involved. One stated subsequent variations of the theme and demonstrated the direction chosen by the case in point. One ended with an evaluation, perhaps a prediction. It had to be informative, philosophic, succinct. I found it very satisfying to write "decisions," and I would read the texts aloud to myself, eliminating the citations, to see if the sentences balanced each other and thrust the reader forward to an inevitable conclusion. The "note," of course, was longer, an essay on a legal topic bristling with footnotes, but there was still the art of turning each footnote into another small "decision."

I was elected an editor, and later a managing editor, of the review. I was in charge of the book section, which gave me the opportunity to read books on general legal topics and to review them. But the great joy was in managing the magazine with a small group of congenial friends. Esprit de corps was a novel experience for me. And always behind the editorial work was my happy little feeling that here was the real world, a man's world, and that I was part of it and liked being part of it. There seemed no reason any more to suppose that even a lawyer's life might not be an enjoyable one. The disastrous first year of World War II had coincided with my second year in Virginia, ending with the fall of France, and although this had added new and horrid apprehensions to daily life, nothing could quite smother the satisfaction that I felt in fitting my new professional key into the lock of a hitherto grimly closed gate.

Further assurance was gained in the summer of 1940 when, instead of returning to fiction, I worked as a "summer boarder" in Sullivan & Cromwell at 48 Wall Street in New York. It was there that I first became interested in the administration of decedents' estates. It is probably not a coincidence that my work has been largely with people and personal problems: planning of wills, of estates, setting up trusts, handling marital separations, divorces, as opposed to the more impersonal matters of corporate or municipal financing. But I was to see the time come when both "corporate" and "personal" work would be almost merged in the great sea of taxation and the practice of law evolve into something more like accounting.

Sullivan & Cromwell offered me a permanent job on my graduation, and I accepted it. I had been fascinated by my summer glimpse into the workings of a great firm. It was at once clear to me that such institutions were completely dependent on the legal aptitudes of their partners and clerks. For no client will long leave his affairs in incompetent hands because of a social or political connection. The firm's whole inventory must consist of brains and character. I was proud to be starting in a job where social qualifications counted for so little and which I had obtained by my own aptitude in a profession not originally selected by inclination.

PHONY WAR

THERE HAD ALWAYS lurked in the back of my mind an uneasy
sense that over and above the tests of manhood that school
and Wall Street were bound to provide, there might lie in wait
an even rougher and more elementary one: that of war. Because my father and his generation had had to shoulder arms
after the completion of their professional education, it seemed
to be in the cards that my generation might also. There was, of
course, my grandfather's age group, which had been as immune
as favored females from the rigors of military service, but that,
no doubt, was the rule-proving exception. And, of course,
things turned out just as I had gloomily prognosticated. If I
had not skipped my senior year at Yale (a fact which some of
my friends now attributed to an uncanny power of vaticina-
tion) I should not have been able to acquire my law degree
and a job before being swept up in World War II.

I detested the idea of war, not only because I feared to be
killed or maimed, but because military life seemed of all lives
the most incompatible. I felt incapable of giving orders and
averse to receiving them. I was hopeless with machinery; I had

never been able to hit a target with a gun. And I abominated the close community living of a barracks, which I associated with the least happy of my Groton years. My loathing of all states of belligerence colored my international thinking and made me favor the isolationist viewpoint. I attended rallies of such organizations as "America First." It was not quite honest, for, deep down in my heart, I had a guilty feeling that we should all be out fighting Hitler.

By the time I went to work for Sullivan & Cromwell as a regular associate in the summer of 1941, it was obvious that I should have to enlist or be drafted, so I applied for a commission in naval intelligence, in the vague hope that this might combine comfort with some degree of utility. Intelligence commissions, so far as I could gather, did not necessitate any tough drill or training. The idea of safety may have also been in the back of my mind, but I did not then anticipate that we should so soon be in a fighting war, and I was primarily interested in dodging the draft. I was not gratified, therefore, to find that I had incurred criticism among my friends and family for seeking a "desk job." Even Mother was bothered. Although an ardent isolationist, desperately apprehensive of the approach of a war which threatened to make hash of all her efforts to keep her sons from physical danger, she could still recognize that physical dangers were not the only kind. What was more dangerous than the scorn of the tribe for a youth who did not aspire to be a brave? But I had made my application, and I stuck to it. Anything else seemed complicated and fussy.

By October, however, it began to look as if we might get into the war, after all, and I concluded that I had made a mistake, not only socially but morally. I attempted to have my application for a commission as an ensign IVS (Intelligence Volunteer Special) changed to one as an ensign DVG (Deck Volunteer General). It was no easy matter. I had to put in for midshipmen's school on the USS *Prairie State*, and to qualify for it, I had to take a night course in trigonometry. With this added to a clerk's hours in Sullivan & Cromwell, the fall of 1941 was a busy one indeed. Yet it was of no avail because the attack on Pearl Harbor occurred before I had been admitted to the *Prairie State*, and on Monday, December 8, I was ordered to report for duty in the Naval Intelligence Office at 50 Church Street to work as a "special agent," checking the records of other applicants for intelligence commissions until my own came through. When it did so, two months later, it was accompanied by orders to the Panama Canal Zone. I protested that I had an application pending for midshipmen's school, but I was advised that to insist on this would look like an attempt to evade overseas duty. The next thing I knew I was on board a naval transport vessel getting under way in Norfolk. Only a few hours later the escorting destroyers dropped their first depth charges. Here I was, plummeted into a shooting war, totally unequipped, with nobody but myself to thank! I felt a prime idiot.

For some fifteen months I was stationed in the headquarters of the Fifteenth Naval District in Balboa. It was my first brush with bureaucracy, and I learned what one can only learn by direct experience: its almost incredible grotesqueness. Was it really possible that in a war — and one that was still being lost — the officer in charge of our division could have ordered all copies of a fifty-page report to be destroyed and the report retyped because it was on the wrong-sized paper? Could a group of officers really have been delegated to supervise the passenger lists of planes landing in the Zone en route to South America to see if anyone on board had ever employed a Japanese servant? Did I dream that a lieutenant who believed that he could locate German submarines by second sight was seriously, and for months, consulted by the admiral and the operations chief? Did I actually spend a week investigating whether or not the commander of a patrol boat, whose job was coveted by my boss, had had a woman in his cabin overnight? No, life in the shore-based navy of Panama could not be satirized, as I discovered, years later, in writing *The Indifferent Children.*

It seems funny enough now, but in 1942, sitting by the Canal as one's friends passed through it on their way to battle in the Pacific, it was simply sickening. I learned to be thankful for the days when the intelligence office accomplished nothing, as opposed to those when it actively (if microscopically) impeded the war effort. I learned to hate the smug, conceited officer-bureaucrats who cared only for their comfort and safety, their drinks and their Panamanian girls friends, and to hate myself for having played my cards in such a way as to be caught among them. I found some slight solace in acting as defense counsel in courts-martial, but very little, for the alliance between the prosecution and court, and the usually obvious guilt of the defendant, picked up drunk by a sober shore patrol, reduced my role to merely making a plea of extenuating circumstances. It never occurred to me to go back to writing, for I could not visualize a future. The war blocked it out. Some experts said it might last ten years. I took night courses in navigation, still in the quest of my DVG rating, but all applications for sea duty were consistently rejected. The district intelligence officer, faithful to his trade of bureaucrat, wished to swell, rather than diminish, his useless staff. His position in the hierarchy depended on the number of his lackeys.

It was in Panama that I began to read fiction for no reason other than my own salvation. I did not have a grade to make, a review to write, a person to talk to, or even an opinion to formulate. I was alone with Henry James, and this was the time that I learned to love the late style, the last novels and the memoirs, and to take in what E. M. Forster has so rightly described as the "unique aesthetic experience" of *The Ambassadors* and *The Golden Bowl.* I began to look back beyond Panama, beyond Virginia, to my Yale days and to wonder if I had not been a fool to cut short what Mother had called my "impractical" courses. Impractical! What in God's name did I have left but literature?

Ultimately the need for officers at sea began to penetrate even the cloistered cells of the Fifteenth Naval District, and I was sent off at last on a two-week convoy to Guantánamo on the USS *Jade*, a converted yacht. On the bridge in the midwatch, during a howling gale, the officer of the deck asked me sarcastically if I did not regret my desk in Balboa. He was surprised at the passion of my denial. I had, of course, to go back to that desk, but now it was not for long. My classification had been changed, and I found myself assigned one morning to another converted yacht, the USS *Moonstone*, as gunnery officer! It was all right. There was nothing to fire at and little to fire with.

Now followed a bizarre year. I had fought free of the IVS category, but not of the Fifteenth Naval District. I had attained the longed-for status of sea duty, but I was still not to be allowed to participate in the war. There was a decided Gilbert and Sullivan note to the navy in the Caribbean, even if an occasional German torpedo shattered a chorus. The *Moonstone*, continually afflicted with engine trouble, would drop out of convoy and spend long, lazy periods of repair in such pleasant ports as Kingston. Eventually we were sent down to Guayaquil to train Ecuadorian midshipmen as part of the State Department "Good Neighbor" program. From there the ship was sent to the Charleston Navy Yard for extensive repairs preparatory to its being given as a present to the Ecuadorian navy. I took advantage of this period to attend the Submarine Chaser School in Miami, but when I graduated and was about to be transferred to a destroyer escort in the "real" navy, the long remorseless arm of the Fifteenth Naval District plucked me back at the last minute, and I had to return to Panama on the *Moonstone*.

Ecuador refused us, even as a gift, despite the repairs, and we became a ship without a country. We were sent from port to port, traveling alone. We arrived in Key West. Could they use us in the Sound School? No. We returned to Charleston. Did they need a shore patrol boat? Move on! We headed north. One night we passed a merchant ship which refused to answer our challenge, and our captain, frustrated with inactivity and high-handed treatment, ordered our three-inch fifty trained on her. Through my binoculars in the moonlight I could make out what was obviously a United States navy gun crew training a five-inch gun on us. The captain, of course, was perfectly right. The challenge had not been answered, and we should have opened fire. But everyone knew how sloppy the merchant marine could be, and there was that five-inch gun ready to blow us out of the water. Hardly in the tradition of Stephen Decatur, I implored the captain to desist. He finally did so, and the merchant ship passed on. Maybe she was a disguised German raider. But we were still in *Pinafore*.

At last the Section Base at Cape May, New Jersey, accepted the *Moonstone* as a patrol boat, and we had a home. I was temporarily detached to take a sound course, and while I was in Washington, the *Moonstone*, on her first mission, collided with a United States destroyer and sank. Only one man was killed in the accident, but there was a good deal of embarrassment and bad feeling. That I had not been aboard the *Moonstone* in her final anguish seemed to put the ultimate touch on my sense of wartime unreality. I joined the survivors in the Brooklyn Navy Yard and arranged for the funeral service of the poor man who had died, a black steward's mate, oldest of the crew, who had succumbed in the water to a heart attack. Referring his soul to the Almighty, the chaplain called him by a wrong name.

But at least I was free now of the adhesive clasping of the Fifteenth Naval District. My application for amphibious duty

95

was promptly accepted, and I was sent to Camp Bradford, Virginia, to be trained. I had seen the first landing ships when they had transited the Canal, and they had struck me as the only vessels on which I might learn to be at home. They were slow and clumsy and required no great expertise. They seemed to make up a consolingly un-naval navy. And indeed so they were to prove.

LESS PHONY WAR

AFTER A COURSE of amphibious training at Camp Bradford, I went, as executive officer, with the captain and crew of the LST 980, to join our ship which was to be commissioned in Boston. The captain was an ex-chief quartermaster of the regular navy, and his dislike and distrust of his junior officers, mostly college graduates and "ninety-day wonders," can be imagined. Although in some ways a decent and oddly charming man, he was riddled with a sense of social inferiority which he took out on us in abuse, in petty persecutions, in constant unreasonable demands and orders. In time the mutual dislike between him and us, exacerbated by a hundred *Caine Mutiny* incidents, flared into something closer to hate. Our revenge was the only one available to juniors: to isolate him. One young ensign who joined the ship some months later came to my cabin to ask me why nobody would speak to him in the wardroom. "I believe you went on liberty with the captain," was my terse reply. It was all very small, but men get small, penned up together for months on end. The perennial problem of the navy is much more Captain Queeg than Captain Bligh.

97

In Boston I began what has been a minor subchapter, or perhaps footnote, to my literary career. I made my first purchase as a collector of rare books. I had quite a bit of cash, for I had banked almost all my navy pay in Panama, and at Goodspeed's I spied a set of Jane Austen, mostly in first edition. I decided all of a sudden that I wanted these more than anything in the world and that I wanted them on board my ship. It seemed to me that if I were drowned or blown up, they would somehow be a consolation. Still, I could not make up my mind to pay the price, and when the ship sailed down to the Chesapeake for its shakedown cruise, I was still without the books. But one day at noon I telephoned George Goodspeed in a burst of resolution from Virginia and asked him to ship the set to me. He did so, but they were lost in the mail. I was heartbroken. The insurance meant nothing to me. I cared only for the books, and when we sailed for Europe, I gave more thought to the Jane Austen I was leaving behind than to my parents. Years later I was to duplicate the set, but, of course, at a far greater price. I had been bitten by the bug, and I was now, for better or worse, a book collector. It is a curious mania, instantly understood by every other collector and almost incomprehensible to the uncontaminated. It is not fundamentally an attractive vice, for its joy is tightly bound up to that of the miser—it depends not only on possession but on title. The true collector cannot bear to borrow or to have his ownership in any way limited, even if it be to a life estate. The treasure must be his, and his alone, like a gold piece fondled behind a locked door.

In the Chesapeake we practiced beaching the ship. To a reserve officer, heading at flank speed toward the shore and feeling the rich, surging impact of the bow on sand was great fun, but to the few Annapolis graduates engaged in the exercises it was acutely painful. The approaching shoreline must have represented to them the ultimate nightmare, and I remember how our group commander would avert his eyes in instinctive recoil as we struck the beach. But then his relegation to the amphibious navy must in itself have been a partial disgrace. We were definitely a second-class fleet, and the battleship *New York*, proceeding down the Chesapeake, signaled to him: "Get your trash out of my way."

The LST 980 arrived in Plymouth, England, in the late winter of 1944, and after some weeks of exercises in the channel, we proceeded through the Strait of Dover and north to the Thames where we anchored near Tilbury Docks. London in that preinvasion spring seemed full of color and gaiety. Uniforms of different nations abounded, and the air was charged with excitement and a tense anticipation. I felt smug with some of the old friends that I met, for, unlike them, I knew all the plans for the invasion. With what still seems to me incredible folly the navy believed that every officer of an amphibious vessel had to be apprised of every detail of the operation, instead of being told simply to "follow the leader," as the similar British units were. After one of our flotilla conferences in Tilbury, an old janitor at the base came hobbling after the departing officers with some papers which had been left on the table. They contained the entire plan for the Normandy landings! How this was kept secret from German intelligence agents must remain one of the mysteries of the war. I imagine that it never occurred to the spies that they could find what they wanted simply by hanging around the docks. They may have been too subtle for their job.

Loaded with British and Canadian troops we sailed for Southampton whence we departed for France on June 6. To me the whole thing had rather the air of a regatta. The long lines of unmolested ships seemed formidable, handsome, valiant; the waves were crisp and blue, the men eager. We saw no enemy craft, no enemy planes. And there was an electric sense of the whole world being there. Two days after the landings King

George VI arrived on the *Aresthusa*, and Mr. Churchill flew overhead in a bomber with a large fighter escort. One of our crew looking up was heard to say: "It must be Clark Gable, on one of his missions." Surely, the enthusiasm of so many hundreds of thousands had to prevail against a Germany gorged with plunder and weakened by sin!

But soon after the invasion the bright colors in which I had fatuously conceived it were all blown away. One night, while the LST 980 was anchored off Gold Beach, waiting to disembark troops, she was struck by three bombs dropped from a low flying German plane. Two crashed through bulkheads into the water; the third lodged in an ammunition truck, one of several such on the tank deck. Obviously, since I live to tell the tale, it did not go off. We were lucky enough to have a British demolition squad among our passengers, the officer in charge of which said to me, with scrupulous good manners, as I was gloomily inspecting the protruding end of the shell: "I realize it's your bomb, sir, but considering how closely we're all concerned, I wonder if you would allow me to take care of it." I never surrendered title to anything more willingly. The bomb was removed with infinite skill and lowered in the sea, but it took with it the last element of my "regatta" atmosphere.

We now operated a shuttle ferry. We crossed and recrossed the Channel, docking in Portland, Southampton, or London, picking up troops, medical units, and even, as the front moved away from the beaches, entertainment groups, and bringing back the wounded and prisoners — thousands of prisoners. Most pathetic among the latter were the Russians, captured by the Germans on the Eastern Front and forced into their western armies. These poor creatures sometimes spoke no dialect known to us and had no idea where or whom they were supposed to be fighting. After loading the tank deck on a Normandy beach we would have to wait for high tide to retract. Sometimes in these delays, when the fighting was still close enough, officers

100

who had come over with us would return for a quick cleanup. I remember one angry British captain, his face caked with mud, pulling open the curtain of the wardroom where I was playing bridge and screaming "Jesus!" as he heard me bid: "Four no trump." He had come out of hell, only a few miles inland.

I think it was this incident which made me and another officer reconsider how we would occupy the long hours of waiting on beaches, at docks, at anchor. My friend was Chauncey Medberry, now chairman of the board of the Bank of America, then an ensign and communications officer of the LST 980. I had two copies of a "Complete Plays of Shakespeare," and I suggested that we read *Macbeth* aloud. Chauncey had a surprising answer. He said that he hated doing things in part and that he would read with me only on condition that I undertook to read all thirty-seven plays, including *Titus Andronicus* and the three parts of *Henry VI.* I was quite willing, and we started, reading in turn, not according to role but speech by speech. We would do this any time we had a few minutes, on the bridge, in the wardroom, in our cabins. At first I was a bit self-conscious when other officers or passengers would peer over our shoulders to find out what the hell we were up to, but Chauncey never was. He had purchased a third Shakespeare in Southampton, and he would simply hand it, open at the correct page, to anyone who lingered beyond a few minutes, asking him to join in. Indeed, one of our officers, who read very slowly and inarticulately, became something of a problem to our sessions.

We read all of Shakespeare, all of Marlowe, and a good deal of Beaumont and Fletcher in the course of the next nine months. Despite the Battle of the Bulge and the buzz bombs, the cold, foggy winter of 1944–1945 still echoes in my mind with iambic pentameter. Chauncey and I were keen enough about our aesthetic solution to the ennui of war to try to proselytize others. He organized discussion groups with the crew; I took volunteers to visit landmarks near our home ports, such as Salisbury Cathedral or Stonehenge. Neither of us had much success. But I remember the charming courtesy of the verger of Salisbury Cathedral, a gas victim from the first war, who, in a valiant attempt to explain a second visit to the cathedral made by two rather Philistine young officers from my ship, offered this suggestion:

"You see, Salisbury is unique among English cathedrals in that it was entirely constructed within a period of twenty-five years. This gives it a purity of Gothic form which the natural good taste of your American boys at once picked up."

I wondered. But I was to think of his kindness a bit ruefully, a year later, when the entire crew of another LST signed up for a tour of the ruins of Nagasaki. There is something about total destruction that is intriguing to American youth.

The LST 980 sustained damage to her hull from a rocky beach in Le Havre which kept her out of the invasion of southern France and ultimately led to her being ordered home. The captain thought that we might now be eligible for shore duty. For me, even after two years, the memory of Panama was sufficiently vivid to make any war zone preferable to any desk job. It was not bravery; it was simply blind horror of the idea of being even ostensibly one of those atrocious bureaucrats who pared their fingernails and read *Life* and *Time* while men died. In much the same way, when I read accounts during the Nuremberg trials of Nazi atrocities in concentration camps, my nightmare was always of being a guard, not a victim. So I applied for command of an LST in the Pacific, and before we had even arrived in Norfolk, I received a message, relayed in blinking lights from the escort commander, that I was to be detached on arrival and to proceed to San Francisco for further orders.

My joy at being relieved at last from my carping, bickering

skipper was intensified by a last-minute triumph. Later I was to incorporate it into a short story for the New Yorker ironically entitled "Loyalty Up and Loyalty Down," but I shall tell it here, for it illustrates the pettiness of wartime obsessions. The convoy commodore, a naval commander, rode the LST 980 on the Atlantic crossing from Plymouth to Norfolk, and I was designated his navigator. This gave me a certain independence of my captain which I abused whenever possible. Every time he sent for me, I would send back word that I was engaged in navigation with the convoy commodore. Fortunately for the convoy, we checked our noon position each day with the escort commander, and I would substitute his for mine. This was only sensible, since he was operating on loran, and his position was exact.

The winter Atlantic was frightful, and our crossing took more than thirty days, more than Columbus took on his fourth and final voyage. One morning in the chart room, as the ship rolled and pitched, the commander steadied himself by catching hold of the side of an open doorway. I saw that the heavy door was loose and swinging. I shouted at him, but he only looked at me, and as he did so, the door closed, shearing his thumb away as a razor might cut through a piece of rope. When his doctor came up and saw my green expression, he hurried to me. The commander growled:

"There's nothing wrong with him. See what you can do about my hand."

The commander was a very brave man, but when his wound had been bound and dressed, it throbbed agonizingly, and this, added to the tempestuous weather, put him in an ugly temper for the next few days. Our captain was so afraid of him that he hugged his cabin, which made life more agreeable for all. And now occurred the incident which gave me my chance. On a stormy night, coming up on the bridge to check our course during the mid-watch, I had a curious sense that something was wrong. Staring ahead through my binoculars, I thought I could make out a ship dead ahead. When I had checked the radar and compasses, it was at once clear what had happened. The gyrocompass had failed, and as it had spun the helmsman had turned the ship slowly to a course 180° from the convoy course. We were headed directly back toward the second ship in our column!

I relieved the officer of the deck and ordered the helmsman to come hard right. In that sea the turn broke every piece of crockery on the ship. It also flung the captain from his bunk to the deck, and he hurried up to the bridge in a fury. Why had I not requested permission to change course? I replied that there had not been time. In a tantrum he forbade me ever again to relieve the officer of the deck. If the officer of the deck saw fit to take my navigational advice, it would be up to him to request permission of the commanding officer to change course. The captain soon forgot his silly tantrum and sillier mandate. I did not.

In the early morning of our expected landfall I was on the bridge watching for the first sea buoy at Norfolk. We were not accustomed to loran, and to pick up a buoy, as I now did with my binoculars, after thirty days of tumultuous seas, at precisely the time and angle that our charted position led us to anticipate, struck me as nothing short of miraculous. But as we drew closer to that wailing buoy, a less exalted idea occurred to me.

There was a distinct set, and the officer of the deck was not compensating for it. On his present course he would probably hit the sea buoy. I called out a suggested course change in a deliberately snotty, superior tone. It was ignored. The officer knew that I had been disempowered, and he was inclined to be stubborn. My tone was just right to fix him in his determination. I now called out suggested course changes loudly every five minutes and insisted that they be entered in the log.

The officer of the deck blandly ignored me. When he at last took in the effect of the set, it was too late. He turned desperately to the right, but we were borne down ineluctably on the buoy whose wail seemed to mock him.

Chauncey and I rushed delightedly to the radar as we heard the heavy booming of the buoy against our bottom. We saw the black dot reappear on the screen and then disappear under the bigger dot of the next LST in column. We were leading the whole convoy over it! On the bridge the captain, black-faced, was being gloriously bawled out by the irate convoy commodore. A year of petty persecutions had been revenged.

But even in false triumph, even in this fetid bottom of my swamp of wartime animosities, I was not quite so blind as to feel no shame. That buoy might easily have damaged the screws of the ships that passed over it. And I had had the gall to criticize the fools in the Panama Canal Zone for impeding the war effort! I saw now what the claustrophobic atmosphere of the LST had produced in me. All I can say in retrospect is that without Shakespeare it might have been even worse.

Changing oceans was like changing navies. In the European theater the army and air force were everything; the navy, only a police escort. And the amphibious navy was even lower than that. In Southampton the army officers' club would not even admit us. Never shall I forget my first glimpse of the Pacific navy in the atoll Ulithi where the lines of battleships, cruisers, carriers, and auxiliary vessels seemed to stretch out to the crack of doom — Japan's doom, anyway. I wondered if those military men in Tokyo had been crazed to think that they could fight such might. Yet I supposed that the great bulk of the craft that I saw that day from the plane had been constructed after the attack on Pearl Harbor.

The LST 130, my first and last command, was a tired veteran of the Pacific war. The officers and crew were too bored even to bother resenting a new skipper from the despised

European theater. I was smart enough to leave things pretty much the way I found them, and I concentrated on preserving the status quo. I had had the needed training as an executive officer except in one thing: ship handling. I could navigate; I could beach the ship; I could direct the drills; I could handle the paper work and take care of the discipline. But in coming alongside a dock or another ship, I was clumsy, and this, unhappily, is the essence of a skipper's job. I dreaded my first mooring alongside another craft, and when it happened it turned out just as badly as I had feared.

On a bright clear afternoon in Ulithi I received orders from the group commander to moor alongside an auxiliary vessel, an APA, to take on water. I got under way and was making my approach when a perverse little breeze sprang up whose effect on the ship I could not seem to gauge. I made two approaches to the APA and had to turn off each time. In my second withdrawal I struck the starboard quarter of my ship against the APA's bow with a resounding crack. The damage was slight, but the accident was inexcusable. I could hear the guffaws of the crews of both ships and the angry squawking of the APA's skipper through his loudspeaker. I turned to the navigator, who had been, I thought, unfriendly to me, and said: "Tell me how to do it." He told me, very precisely, in front of the bridge gang, and we made a successful mooring.

It was awful. I stood convicted before my crew of impotence. A few years later I was to use the incident in a short story called "The Fall of a Sparrow." There the LST captain is destroyed by the experience. He isolates himself in his cabin and takes to the bottle. But he, of course, had to be shown as an abnormally weak man. What got me through the incident was the catharsis of acknowledging to the officers in the wardroom that night that I couldn't have made the mooring alone. This elementary bit of courtesy and justice helped to restore my confidence in myself. It did not help me much with the officers, but none of them gave a damn, anyway, how bad a ship handler I was. A commanding officer of an amphibious vessel in World War II did not need the admiration of his crew. All he needed was their obedience, and he had that by simple reason of his position. But *I* was helped by my candor. I felt better the moment I could say to myself: "All right, you're a bum ship handler, a mediocre officer. What of it? If the navy could have got someone better, they would have. Look at what the skipper of LST ———— did to *his* ship the other day. What is an LST but a sea truck, and how well does a truck have to be driven?" The LST 130 hardly needed a John Paul Jones.

My Pacific life after this was peaceful but dull. We returned to the United States for repairs, and while we were in California, the war ended. So great was my relief that I hardly minded when I discovered that I still had to take the ship to Japan. I had "made the grade" — however much by the skin of my teeth — and America had made the grade. Nothing that happened hereafter could matter too much. Sailing into Sasebo harbor, past the half-sunken hulks of Japanese war vessels, I did not even wait for a pilot. I was a lawyer; I was an amphibious officer; I was a member of the winning team! I had shown myself I could live in the "real world."

And I was writing again. This always happened whenever I gained confidence in myself. As soon as I thought I was standing on the particular step on which I "ought" to be standing in the moving stairway of life, and had a little time, I would start to write. In the last two years of law school I had felt on the right step, but the *Law Review* had provided a substitute for writing. And in the first two years of the war I had felt a fraud and a failure and could not have written a word of fiction. But with a happy sense of belonging in the amphibious world, with long idle days, swinging at anchor in this or that atoll, and with the reemergence at last of a future in which

107

one might possibly even publish what one had written, I started to write *The Indifferent Children.*

My idea was to re-create Beverly Stregelinus as the most ridiculous young man in the world and introduce him to Audrey, the heroine of my first novel. I would then throw them both into the war and see if I could redeem them. Audrey became a "Zonite," a member of a Panama Canal Zone family, a perfect atmosphere for her. What would she not do to escape from the smallness, the meanness, the humidity of such a life? Beverly, for his part, would be a perfect foil for the Naval Intelligence Office, making it even sillier by the shrillness of his sense of its silliness. In the end I was to find that I could not do much with anyone as silly as Beverly so I threw a buzz bomb at him while he was on liberty from an LST in London. But the satisfaction that I derived in writing the chapters on the intelligence office in Balboa was so keen that for a time I almost wondered if the longed for return to civilian life and to Sullivan & Cromwell might not be coming too soon.

At Guam I at last received orders detaching me from the LST 130 and sending me to the United States on an APA. It was a strange and delectable feeling to be a passenger again. But it turned out that I had one final duty. I was singled out of a group of officers in Portland and placed in charge of a troop train carrying three thousand sailors to New York City. Christmas was approaching, the war was over; the men, although still in the navy, considered themselves civilians. The disciplinary problems can be imagined. In the long cold trip the breakdown of heating and lighting in some of the cars did not help. Liquor, though forbidden, abounded. At first, like a good lieutenant, I insisted on making my morning and evening inspection of the entire train. I would have done this to the end had I not been saved by a politic group of chief petty officers.

In the navy these represent a necessary compromise between

the hard-nosed idealism of the regular officers and the more natural simplicity of the enlisted men. Sly, cynical, unimpressed, shoulder-shrugging, they address themselves, like eunuchs in an Eastern court, to the basic machinery of government. The delegation which came to my stateroom pointed out to me politely that if I continued to inspect the train, it was only a matter of time before I was knocked over the head with a bottle. This would be a mutiny; the train would be stopped; nobody, including the chiefs, would get home for Christmas. Would I agree to let them run the train? We worked it out that I would stay in my stateroom and receive their reports, like an oriental potentate in a forbidden city, from behind a closed door. Most appropriately, I had in my bag, as reading material for the trip, some volumes of Gibbon.

In my isolation on that rowdy train, on those dull frigid days, I did a lot of thinking. All of my small, puffy pride at being the skipper of a tiny unit in a great nation victorious over the forces of evil seemed to blow away before the drunken racket of those three thousand men. What is the sense of inferiority, born so deep in the would-be intellectual of the twentieth century, which makes him respect animal behavior as if it were possessed of some greater reality? Why did I have to assume that everything from which I naturally recoiled had to have a greater validity in the scheme of things than anything which attracted me? Why did I feel that anyone on that train was a wit more "fundamental" than I was?

I brooded over the four war years. I had served in two oceans. I had seen petty bureaucrats obsessed with their trivial bickering in the damp heat of Central America. I had seen violent storms and submarine attacks in the Atlantic. I had watched London under the buzz bombs. I had sat on the tank deck of a ship loaded with ammunition watching while a bomb demolition squad, a few feet away, with fingers moving so slowly that they seemed to be still, had inched an unexploded shell out of a truck and lowered it into the sea on a sick bay stretcher. I had seen German nurses, prisoners, come on board our ship screeching "Heil Hitler" and had sat with one of them who had swallowed poison while a pharmacist's mate tried to save her. I had driven in a jeep through the atomized ruins of Nagasaki. And what did it all amount to? Had I ever really been away from home? Had I once been scratched? Had I gone a single day without three meals? Had I gone a single day without shaving?

Some time later I came across a passage in a book by Henry de Montherlant which seemed exactly to fit me:

"Some men seem to repudiate the tragic. In small things as well as great. There is a street accident; they are never there to see it. Bombs and shells can swirl about them; they are never touched. It is not that they are more timid than others or even that they keep themselves in the shelter. On the contrary, they may have a yearning for the tragic test. It makes no matter: drama never strikes where they are. They go through wars and revolutions without ever seeing a corpse, without ever really taking in what it is that turns a man into a corpse. They are always safely preserved — bourgeois in spite of themselves."

And so what? That was what I was beginning to ask myself in that long train ride home. Wasn't the bourgeois as real as the Hemingway or Montherlant hero? If you prick him, will he not bleed? If you tickle him, will he not laugh? Was there any point, in the one life that he was given, for him to fuss over what he was not? Oh, how obvious these conclusions seem! And yet a man can spend his whole existence never learning the simple lesson that he has only one life and that if he fails to do what he wants with it, nobody else really cares. As my train approached New York, I had a sense of jubilation at all that was over and at all that lay before me. I thought I might have achieved some kind of independence from my ghosts. I didn't know it then, but I had a long way still to go.

The officers who met the train were horrified at the state in which they found it. They suggested that there had been drinking on board and threatened me with a formal investigation. But when they received the report of the muster of the men, their expressions suddenly changed. The muster was complete. Not one man was missing! Every other train had lost at least a dozen crossing the continent, because men got off at the stops. How had I managed to accomplish my remarkable feat?

"They were too drunk to get off," was all I could mutter.

THE INDIFFERENT CHILDREN

RELEASED FROM ACTIVE DUTY, I took a vacation before returning to Sullivan & Cromwell during which I worked feverishly
to finish my novel. I had a feeling of "last chance" about it.
The old life, which I had thought might never come back, was
back with a vengeance. I even envied my contemporaries who
were returning to law school to complete their third and final
year. It seemed to me that the war had swept away my legal
education, and that, coming back to Wall Street, I should be
an actor who has forgotten his lines. But if I should have a
novel finished, a novel submitted, a novel (dream of dreams!)
even published, I should then have an amulet from the magic
world of letters which I could carry in my pocket for luck and
finger lovingly through the long years of a business and legal
reality.

And indeed so at first it proved. I found the work at Sullivan & Cromwell very difficult to pick up again; I needed the
assistance of night lectures at the Practicing Law Institute. I
worked hard and tensely, and when I was inclined to feel too
sorry for myself, I would think of my almost completed book

and build fantasies in my mind of the great success it might one day enjoy. I was soon to discover, however, that as I regained my stride in the office, the law and the novel began to exchange functions. The question of publication became the problem, and my law practice the consolation.

My friend James Oliver Brown was an editor of Little, Brown and Company, and it was to him that I submitted the manuscript. Two readers at his firm showed considerable interest in the book, but there was not enough enthusiasm in the end for publication. Later, Jim was to abandon publishing and become a literary agent, in which capacity he has been of incalculable help to me through the years, but at that time there was no more he could do. I sent the manuscript to another friend, Henry James (I liked the name) at Prentice-Hall. To my great excitement it was accepted, and publication was planned for early in 1947.

But now began a serious argument with my parents. Mother felt that I might one day write a better book, and she was strongly of the opinion that *The Indifferent Children* would not be an auspicious start to a literary career. Father, I think, suspected that I was not going to have a literary career at all, and he feared that the quixotic appearance of a single novel would do me little good with the partners of Sullivan & Cromwell. And both of them apprehended that the sections of the book which dealt with New York social life would be viewed with derision by our world. I was living with my parents at the time, and the pressure to which I was subjected was intense. Ultimately, I agreed to publish the novel under a pseudonym, and, with some bitter irony, I selected that of "Andrew Lee." He was a clerical ancestor of Mother's who was supposed to have cursed any of his descendants who should drink or smoke.

The reader may be surprised that at the age of twenty-nine and the veteran of a world war, I should have been so subject to the parental yoke. The answer was that I shared their point of view. I had no wish to have my law career damaged, and I had Mother's dread of the frowns and snickers of friends. But this did not keep me from resenting their failure to put on blinders to avoid seeing the things which all three of us imagined that we saw. I wanted them to show more pride in the fact that I had got the novel accepted at all. I wanted them to be more emotionally and less judiciously on my side.

Since this memoir will not go beyond a certain point in my life, I must state here that when my parents at last came around, they did so handsomely. When I gave up the law to write — to poor Father's infinite distress — he agreed to support me. And Mother constituted herself my most careful reader and constructive critic. When she was eighty-two years old, she told me exactly what was wrong with the first draft of *I Come as a Thief*, and I altered the scheme of the novel. Even when I started to publish books on subjects acutely painful to them, Father and Mother kept their objections to a minimum. *The Rector of Justin* aroused resentment in the Groton family of which they were close members. *The Embezzler* irritated some of Father's friends and clients who hated to see the ashes of the Richard Whitney scandal raked over. And *The House of Five Talents* was just the kind of inquiry into the extravagance of the rich that Mother found most vulgar. Yet never again were the angry scenes of *The Indifferent Children* reenacted.

When I showed the first printed copy of that novel to my older brother, he said: "Why, it looks like a real book." He was joking, but he expressed precisely what I was thinking. It seemed to me that my literary effort was a basic fraud. I was not *really* a writer. And the pen name cruelly confirmed my sense of guilt. I hadn't dared use my own name! Furthermore, it made me ridiculous, because everyone knew about the book, and nobody could understand the bizarre shyness of this last-minute refusal to acknowledge my own work. Worse still, there were many who thought that I must have libeled actual people and was trying to hide from the consequences. What should have been an exciting debut was hopelessly soured for me. But one review made up for almost everything. At noon in my lunch club, on May 27, 1947, I saw the headline in the *New York Sun* "A Remarkable Novel about the War" and read with incredulity the following passage by William McFee:

"Here is a novelist of the caliber of the Henry James who wrote *Washington Square* and *The Portrait of a Lady* rather than of the author of *The Ambassadors*. It is James alive to our times, aware of things and people James himself never even sensed, but with the psychological alertness and a mastery of English the master would have enjoyed very much indeed."

Although, devoted Jacobite that I was, this comparison struck me as heresy, it pleased me as no line of print had before or has since. That I could write a book about which an author like William McFee could utter such a remark did a great deal to make me indifferent to what people might say or to what I imagined they might say.

I now started writing short stories. I worked at nights, on weekends, even in the office, with a new confidence. Gretchen Finletter, one of Walter Damrosch's daughters and herself an author, spoke to Edward Weeks of the *Atlantic Monthly* about me, and he wrote to ask me for them. He purchased two, "Maud" and "Finish, Good Lady," and I appeared at last in print under my own name. When I put all my stories together in a volume entitled *The Injustice Collectors*, it was rejected by Prentice-Hall but accepted by Houghton Mifflin where my friend Patricia MacManus was then working, and Houghton Mifflin has published my fiction ever since in a long and happy relationship. With the appearance of *The Injustice Collectors*, which had a good press, I began to be known as a writer.

People found it extraordinary that a clerk in a firm with

such a reputation for hard work as Sullivan & Cromwell should be able to turn out books. But the partners themselves seemed to accept my avocation with great good nature. The then senior, John Foster Dulles, used to say to people who protested that he overworked his associates: "On the contrary—they have to fill out the day writing novels." I was not particularly troubled by working at my writing on evenings or weekends, or even at the office if I had a free hour, but I was increasingly bothered by a nagging apprehension that I might be slighting my literary muse by not devoting full time to her. Was it possible — just possible — that I had been born for Parnassus if I dared to scale it?

We have come a long way from the Renaissance when one man was allowed to do many things. The twentieth century is the age of specialization. Union rules require one laborer to turn a tap on, another to turn it off. Academe is equally rigid. And the exaggerated dedication to his art of Henry James, who believed that a novelist should not even marry, has been much admired. I shuddered to think what the Master would have thought of the promiscuity of my two professions. It seemed to me that sooner or later I should have to make a choice between them and put all my eggs in one basket. I did not in the least want to. In the first place, I should be financially dependent on my parents. In the second, I was completely happy now in Sullivan & Cromwell.

I liked everything about the firm, including the hierarchical structure, which struck me as a necessity to assure fairness, continuity, and efficiency in an organization so large. It seemed to me a sort of benevolent navy, where promotion went only by merit and where useless bureaucrats would not be tolerated. Perhaps unconsciously, I emulated my father in transferring a larger part of my emotional life to my office than do most lawyers. I was full of "school spirit" about the firm and even incurred the odium of some of the younger associates, who unlike me were struggling to support wives and children, by telling the managing partner that I considered the postwar salary arrangements handsome to the point of generosity. Yet I was perfectly sincere.

Again like my father, I was as much interested in the firm as in the law. Several of my best friends were associates there. I followed their careers with intense interest, but I did not share their ambition. I had no wish to become a partner. I was Peter Pan. It seemed to me that without the responsibilities of age and partnership, I would be free to be a lawyer and a writer and an observer — oh, yes, always an observer. I remember startling the wife of one of the associates at a Saturday night party (the men worked too hard to go out during the week, but the Saturday parties used to last all night) when I told her that I might eventually give up the law to write. "Eventually!" she exclaimed. "Hadn't you better make up your mind? You're a big boy now." I was upset because it was exactly what I had been trying not to face. I did not want to grow up. The war was over, and I liked things as they were.

It was the atmosphere of these years (1946–1951) that I tried to catch in *The Great World and Timothy Colt*. I was considerably startled to read in the reviews that I was exploring the question of whether or not it was possible for a man to keep his integrity in a Wall Street law firm. I had never seen anyone faced with such a problem in Sullivan & Cromwell. What the critics had not seen (and it still seems obvious to me when I reread the book) is that Timothy Colt's betrayal of his trust is suicidal in nature. A naive, idealistic, and industrious young man, he is faced with a crisis when, utterly exhausted, he at last turns on the client who has been hounding him. The senior partner, his hero, forces Timothy to apologize. Childishly bitter, Timothy then flings himself into the arms of an opposing clique in the firm. But his resentment turns to self-hate when the senior partner suddenly dies. Timothy is now grimly determined to punish himself by becoming all the things that seem to go with his tarnished soul: an adulterer, an opportunist, a false trustee. The critics failed to understand that he had to wrench himself from his habits, his ideals, even his inclinations, to turn himself into a crook. There was no temptation to be one, and, indeed, little opportunity.

Considering all other possible sources of nonwriting income, I now recalled my old idea of the academic life as a basis for a literary career. It seemed to me that teaching English would be less exacting than practicing law, and I went up to New Haven to see Professor Robert French, master of Jonathan Edwards College, of which I had been a member at Yale. I asked him how long it would take me to get a Ph.D. in English literature. Obviously, matters were complicated by my not having a B.A. degree from Yale, but he was very kind and told me how it could be done. He even offered to arrange to make me a fellow of Jonathan Edwards College which would give me the financial assistance of a free room and board. I became very excited and told him that I would take immediate steps to transfer to an academic career. He smiled and then asked me one question which blew my little plan to bits:

"You have trained yourself to one noble profession, and you are already cheating on it. What extraordinary compulsion makes you wish to train yourself in another in order to do the same thing?"

But back at Wall Street I was still unhappy. The burning ambition of the other associates made me feel more and more out of place in our discussions of the future. One friend of mine compiled a study of the existing partners, with all the vital statistics of their ages, financial means, social backgrounds, legal aptitudes, to determine what factors prevailed in the ultimate selection. Yet here was I, secretly praying that I would *not* be a partner, because I had a blurred idea that the dedication of the members to the firm was too sacred a thing to be sullied with any outside interest. And yet I did not want to be passed over, either.

The situation ultimately became impossible. I had to find out, once and for all, what I was. My father, unfailingly kind, told me that he would support me financially in any experiment I chose. Could love go further? At the end of the year 1951, with bitter regret and apprehension, I resigned from Sullivan & Cromwell.

COMPROMISE

ALL OF 1952 and 1953 I devoted to writing. In this period I wrote a novel, *A Law for the Lion*, and the stories which make up *The Romantic Egoists*. I would rise every morning at eight and write in my pajamas and wrapper until noon. I would then shave, dress, and go out for lunch. In the afternoon I would return to my apartment and write until five. I would then read for an hour. In the evenings I usually went out to dinner. I never worked at night.

I learned to type, a practice which I subsequently discontinued. I tried to meet other writers, and largely through Vance and Tina Bourjaily, I to some extent succeeded. Vance was the editor of a pocket book periodical called *Discovery*, the owners of which underwrote his parties for writers. But even before the backing of *Discovery*, he and Tina had organized Sunday afternoon meetings of young writers in a Greenwich Village bar called the White Horse Tavern. There or at Vance's apartment I saw Norman Mailer, Gore Vidal, William Styron, Hortense Calisher, Calder Willingham, Chandler Brossard, Frederick Buechner, Herman Wouk, Merle Miller — there seemed no end to the list. Vance had a keen eye for talent and a large heart.

I suppose there is a self-consciousness inherent in the nature of any literary gathering which tends to inhibit the members. With enough to drink, of course, they form into smaller, more congenial groups who "go on" to one member's apartment or to another bar. The Bourjaily gatherings undoubtedly had great value as starters. My trouble was that I never got beyond the start. The fact that I was a Wall Street lawyer, a registered Republican, and a social registrite was quite enough for half the people at any one party to cross me off as a kind of duck-bill platypus not to be taken seriously. And then, too, I was inclined to be stiff and formal. Hortense Calisher and Gore Vidal were always delightful, always stimulating, but they were far more sophisticated than most of the group. The others largely ignored me. Yet I am sure I had read more books by more of the guests at any one party than anyone else. I did not realize how much I wanted to be included until Norman Mailer congratulated me on a short story entitled "The Gem-like Flame" which had just appeared in a periodical called *New World Writing*. He gave me the only true compliment that one writer can give to another. He said that he would not have minded having written it himself. I was so pleased that I went right home. I wanted to leave one such assembly with a happy impression.

To be totally fair about my experiments with literary milieus, I should admit that I was making them, as with so many other experiments in my life, out of a false sense of duty. But happily I was learning at last to rid myself of this dismal inner companion. Without the pressures of the law I now had time to be psychoanalyzed, and Dr. John M. Cotton was teaching me to comprehend emotionally all the things which I had hitherto understood only intellectually. There were not many surprises in the long probe into my past and childhood, but it made all the difference to me in the world to *feel* free as opposed simply to being aware that I ought to be.

The bearing of this therapy upon my fiction has some importance. John Cotton confirmed my suspicion that a man's background is largely of his own creating. What I took to be important in my past were things very different from what my siblings and cousins may have taken. I daresay that some of them will find almost unrecognizable the background described in this book. This may seem obvious enough, but I have learned over the years, from hundreds of reviews of my more than twenty books, that American critics still place a great emphasis on the effect of background on character, and by background they mean something absolute which is the same for all those in the foreground. Furthermore, they tend to assume that the effect of any class privilege in a background must be deleterious to a character and that the author has introduced such a background only to explain the harm done. Now the truth is that the background of most of my characters has been selected simply because it is a familiar one to me and is hence more available as a model. In most cases, the problems of the characters are personal, or psychological, and would have existed in a multitude of other geographical areas and other social strata.

I cannot but surmise that the stubborn refusal on the part of many critics to see this is evidence of a resentment on their part against the rich, a resentment sometimes carried to the point of denying that a rich man can be a valid subject for fiction. Granville Hicks at times has come close to stating this. Such a point of view would have been, of course, ridiculous in the eighteenth or nineteenth centuries when the great bulk of the characters of fiction came from the upper or upper middle classes. Critics did not resent Anna Karenina or Colonel Newcome. In our times the gaps between social classes have been narrowed to slits which are often difficult to detect, yet it always seems to follow that interclass resentments are intensified as the reasons for them diminish. It is a truism, for example, that blacks are angrier now than they were a century ago. But at least they still have something to be angry about. What to me is tiresome is the abounding resentment of Fraternity B for Fraternity A or of Country Club B for Country Club A.

I attribute much of the great popularity of John O'Hara and John P. Marquand to the fact that both took very seriously this tenacious American illusion in the survival of hierarchies. Their novels are crammed with the minutiae of social distinctions, of who wore what kind of tie or shoe and of who belonged to which set or club. I do not mean to denigrate either novelist; I have read all the works of both with much pleasure and profit. But I still insist that one can see that, however differently dressed or affiliated, their characters all talk in very much the same language and communicate, despite their touchiness, with considerable ease. And that is the way America is. I remember Sidney Lumet telling me, and brilliantly too, everything that I had had in mind in writing *The Rector of Justin*. Never have I had the feeling of being so perfectly understood. But when he added, by way of underlining his own perspicacity, "And my background is one hundred percent the opposite of yours," I failed to see the relevance. There is nothing in *The Rector of Justin* which requires a special background to be understood.

More and more, in my own fiction, the principal characters have come to create their own worlds. My hero in *The Great World and Timothy Colt* lives in a Miltonic universe of good and evil with a compulsion to join the latter. Michael Farish in *Venus in Sparta* inhabits a grim world of phallic symbols. And in *The Embezzler* I viewed the Prime family through the different points of view of Guy and of his wife Angelica. To Guy, the Primes are the last word in Edwardian elegance; to

123

Angelica, they are a vulgar, pushing lot. But the time came when, irked by the insistence of critics and friends that the most important thing in the shaping of my characters had to be their money, I decided that it might be interesting to write the novel that everyone thought I had been writing.

It was not a coincidence that *The House of Five Talents* turned out to be a historical novel, historical at least in the sense that half of its action takes place before 1917, the year of my birth. I simply discovered that I could not write an interesting novel about the effect of an inherited fortune in the present day. The subject cried out for the last century, so I worked out my plot as the story of a great American fortune over a period of four generations. But even at that it was more the story of the money and the things into which it was converted than of the people who hoarded or spent it. *The House of Five Talents* may be the most unusual book I have written, but I wonder if it does not belong more to history than literature. In the end, my old-maid narrator, Augusta Millinder, almost denies the existence of the characters:

"I sometimes think . . . that my family were at all times simple, ordinary people, pursuing simple, ordinary tasks, who stood out from the crowd only in the imagination of those observers who fancied from reading the evening papers that tiaras and opera boxes made an organic difference. Perhaps that is my ultimate discovery of what the money meant, that it meant nothing at all, or, at any rate, very little. But I find such a conclusion oddly disagreeable. It makes me wonder if I should ever have bothered to write these pages at all. It makes me feel no better than a shopgirl who goes to the movies to see Joan Crawford play an heiress and to imagine herself throwing a diamond necklace from the stern of a yacht to satisfy a passing tantrum."

To sum up the account of my nonlegal years, they added

124

nothing to my stature as a writer. The main thing about them, of course, was to have been time, but even that proved an undependable friend. My writing hours increased, but both the quantity and quality of my writing remained the same. Before the end of 1953 I had decided to return to the practice of law and to write thereafter when and where I could.

It was not an easy matter to get started again. I could not go back to Sullivan & Cromwell, for they had a policy against it. I was thirty-six years old. I had no clients. It was reasonable for firms to assume that I had rusted in my quixotic literary interlude. But just as I was becoming discouraged, George Sharp called me. He was a member of Sullivan & Cromwell, but not one to whom I had gone for advice, since I had not worked for him there. He concentrated on my predicament, scanned the field, and found precisely the opening that I needed in my present firm, Hawkins, Delafield & Wood. It was the most disinterested act of Christian charity that I have ever experienced.

Returning to Wall Street in the spring of 1954, I felt that I had come home. I was sure that I would not give up the law again, and indeed I have not. People ask me how I manage to write and practice. Sometimes I think it is the only thing about me that interests them. All I can say is that a great step was taken when I ceased to think of myself as a "lawyer" or a "writer." I simply was doing what I was doing when I did it. But mine is not a career that I should recommend to a young man starting out. It is a peculiar shell that over the years I have managed to manufacture for myself.

Or have I? Wasn't it there from the beginning? Was it not merely a question of clearing away the cobwebs of fears that had obsessed me? And when they were cleared away, was the shell not there, already made? I think that is the more plausible answer. So often men are born with all the tools they need, but are blocked by the simple fear of using them. Yet I suppose that the very act of overcoming that fear may in itself be an indispensable educative process toward using those tools in certain ways. So one never really knows. All a writer can do is tell the story of what led up to his becoming a writer. And that is what I have tried to do.

PART TWO

Influences and Experiments

I have added these three chapters by way of appendixes
because, although they relate directly to the story of how
I became a writer, they do not fit in chronologically with
the events of Part One.

RUTH DRAPER AND
"THE CLUB BEDROOM"

THE ONLY GREAT ARTIST who was an intimate of my family's circle was the monologist Ruth Draper. She lived in the same apartment house as my parents on East 79th Street, and I went frequently to the cocktail parties and musicales which she gave for her many nephews and nieces and younger cousins in the little parlor with the huge map of the world studded with gold stars in the sites of her performances. Of course, I saw her do all her monologues on the stage, some of them many times over, but I also saw her do them at these parties, for it was happily not difficult to persuade her to act. Indeed, it struck me early that she was more natural in her monologues than out of them. Delightful, amusing, and warmhearted as she was, there was a faint air of affectation to the nonacting Ruth Draper which disappeared in that moment of silence which always preceded the transference of herself into one of her characters. The "real" woman was the artist.

I was always entranced with her art. I envied her a magic which she could carry around with her, which had no need of pencil or paper, of brush or fiddle, or even of costume or stage.

129

After that moment of silence, of stillness, there she was: the busy society woman of "The Italian Lesson," keeping all the balls of her hectic life in the air with a juggling skill as rare as it was futile, or the mumbling old Jewish grandmother of "Three Generations in a Court of Domestic Relations," or the compulsively giggling debutante with the need for "uplift" who confides in her young man: "Things mean things to me." How could one woman have had so many faces, so many intonations? How could she speak so many languages?

Yet my study of her art was not altogether uncritical. I noted early that she was at her best when she was satirical, and at her satirical best when she was funny. As a frantic mother at a children's party, as a fatuous gardener whose flowers are never out, as an earnest Boston lady trying to be fair about modern art, she was without peer. But when she touched on the deeper human emotions, on love of child, of country, of lover, she was inclined to be sentimental, even mawkish. This became more apparent when, against the pleas of her friends, including my own, she began, in her later years, to update her monologues. "Vive la France," originally set in World War I, was moved to World War II. The trouble was that the deep sentiment in which the sketch was originally bathed belonged not only to the French patriot woman's plight but to the war fury of the times, which had united all classes in a dedication of hate that even artists and writers regarded as a sacred rage. As such, the monologue was a perfect period piece. Moved to the 1940s it struck a note of shrillness.

Ruth Draper wrote her own monologues, which were published after her death in 1956. Even to those who never saw her they can provide entertainment, for her talent had a distinct literary side. To me she was a living novel of manners. The very perfection of her method of fixing a character in place and in time made the more distressing the desecration of her modernization. For when she updated, she was basically acting another person's piece — usually that of the theatrical agent who had pushed her into it — and that was something she could never do. Even when the great Henry James, who had had the wisdom to advise her never to act in a play with others ("You have woven your little magic carpet — stand on it"), had composed a monologue for her about an American woman dressing to be presented at court, she would never perform it. Her words, like her gestures, had to be her own.

Some years after her death, reading one of her monologues, I was struck by the thought that there ought to be a way in which I could utilize the vivid emotion which this memory aroused. But all that I could think of was to write a monologue myself. After some consideration I succeeded in visualizing Ruth Draper as a Mrs. Ruggles. Mrs. Ruggles was a widow of sixty with two children, a daughter and a son, who were approaching middle age without the least likelihood of ever getting married. The daughter was perversely inclined to have affairs with elderly, married men, the son was homosexual. Mrs. Ruggles's tragedy was that she had no grandchildren to photograph for the kind of family-group Christmas cards preferred by her friends. Then I began to write the monologue. Mrs. Ruggles tells a fellow member of her club about her plan to rent the corner bedroom there, her concept of bliss and luxury and a deliberate self-indulgence to compensate for her lack of posterity, only to discover that the chairman of the house committee whose consent is required is her daughter's lover's wife. But who would publish my monologue? Who would produce it? Who would act it? After much cogitation I decided to convert it into a one-act play with three characters: the widow, the clubwoman, and the widow's daughter.

The gist of my little drama would lie in the widow's relating to the clubwoman the sorry tale which has resulted in her sterile existence and in the unfulfilled lives of her two children. It would thus still be a kind of monologue. In my Yale days I had gone three times in a row to see Nazimova play Mrs. Alving in *Ghosts*. The moment that I had waited for was the scene where Mrs. Alving tells the fatuous pastor the true and horrible story of her marriage. It might have surprised Ibsen that anyone could have found the climax of his play in that moment, but it seemed to me that if he had rung his curtain down then and there, his drama would still have been complete.

With the inspiration of Ruth Draper and Nazimova I wrote *The Club Bedroom* on a single weekend. It was printed in *Esquire* and produced by Channel 13 in New York City and later off Broadway and by countless amateur groups. Although I have written four full-length plays and many television scripts, this little one-act drama has been my sole production. It received only middling reviews, but the exciting thing was that a remarkable actress, Ruth White, saw in Mrs. Ruggles's narration of the facts of her troubled home life to the sympathetic club member the possibility of doing something not unlike what Nazimova had done in *Ghosts*. She received a "Tony" for the part and went on to greater things. There are those who believe that she would have become one of our famous stars. Alas, she died prematurely. I like to feel that I was a link between Ruth Draper and Ruth White.

AMÉLIE RIVES

BEFORE I LEFT for law school a friend of my father's had asked me to call upon the venerable Princess Pierre Troubetzkoy who lived in romantic, impoverished isolation in a decaying manor house, Castle Hill, near Charlottesville, but I had for a time avoided the mission because the Princess, under her maiden name of Amélie Rives, had been a well-known novelist and poet, and all such things I had put firmly behind me. But when I discovered that I liked the law, there seemed less need for such austerity, and I drove out to Cobham on a cool, cloudless November afternoon in 1938 for the cup of tea to which I had been invited.

I could hardly believe the boxwood that lined the narrow driveway. It towered over my Pontiac, thirty feet high, and scratched against the doors on both sides as I drove slowly through it. I learned later that a tree surgeon had warned the Princess that it would die unless treated for a price beyond her means, and she had retorted: "It was planted by a gardener who worked for George II. I think it will last my time — and yours!" It has.

When I emerged at last from the long, green tunnel, I could see, over a ragged strip of lawn shaded by tulip trees, the two-story pink brick façade of a modest, mid-nineteenth-century planter's mansion. Corinthian columns supported a balcony that covered the front door; on either side I could make out similar columned porches. Getting out of my car, I stood for some minutes taking in the house and the lawn. For all its simplicity it exuded an air of unmistakable distinction. It seemed somehow to disdain not only the opulence of a Yankee North, but the opulence of the deeper South. It bespoke the high Jeffersonian fellowship of all the civilized people who had lived there.

When I had been admitted by an old black woman who had finally answered the bell that I could hear tinkling deep within the house, I found still another atmosphere. The simplicity of the exterior was tempered by something more sophisticated, more elegant, within. A wide, noble hall stretched to the back of the mansion, past a circular stairwell, to unite what had once been two houses, the nineteenth-century brick front with the simpler clapboard eighteenth-century rear. The square parlor, to the left of the front door, where I waited for my hostess, echoed the elegant, curlicued Paris of the 1840s where William Cabell Rives, her grandfather, had been minister to Louis-Philippe. A painting over the mantel showed four fancily dressed children, with rather oversized heads, playing in the Tuileries Gardens. I wondered if I would have the legendary midnight experience of the Hollywood producer who, on a visit to Castle Hill to discuss a contract for one of the Princess's novels, had been told by the tiny ghost of a lady in blue crinoline to leave at once and go home. But the little lady whom I now saw in the hall doorway proved to be my hostess.

She was small and straight, with white hair, carefully waved, and with delicately penciled, dark eyebrows. Her features were very fine and regular, her cheekbones high; her face had few wrinkles. Her eyes were large and blue-gray; they were probingly curious and seemed to hide reserves of laughter. One felt that she had been a great beauty in a day when great beauties had been made much of. There was no nonsense about asking why a law student should wish to spend a Saturday afternoon with a woman of seventy-five. The Princess knew well what she was worth.

At tea she wanted to hear about the law school and what was going on at the university. She knew the dean and many of the law faculty and was very funny about them. It was some time before I could bring her to a discussion of things past. After all, she had known Henry James! But when I succeeded, she was fascinating. From the past we went to the occult, for I asked her about the ghosts of Castle Hill and the lady in blue. She told me of a garden party in Rome where she had noticed the guests exclaiming over a strange red bird. She had looked up and seen a Virginia redbird in a tree. It was the harbinger of tragedy in the Rives family, and she had known at once that her ailing mother was dead.

When it seemed time to go, I rose but she asked me to stay for supper.

"But I warn you," she added, "you must pray for the miracle of the loaves and fishes!"

So our friendship began.

*   *   *

Amélie Rives was born in Richmond in 1863. She and I used to agree that if she ever wrote her memoirs, she would have a wonderful opening sentence: "My family was happy in godparents: Lafayette was my father's; General Lee, mine." Her aunt and namesake, another Amélie Rives, had been named for another godparent, Queen Marie-Amélie, consort of Louis-

135

Philippe. And in addition to these there must have been a host of fairy godmothers at young Amélie's cradle in war-torn Virginia, for despite defeat and reconstruction she grew up as the heiress of all that was enchanting in the old South: she had beauty, wit, charm, and inspiration. Many of her contemporaries were to take the last-named quality for genius.

As to many of early developing talents, her greatest successes came at the threshold of her career. At twenty-five she published *The Quick or the Dead?* which seems to have been the *Love Story* of 1888. It posed the question: Can a woman love completely twice? Can a widow remarry and duplicate her earlier happiness? The mild aura of scandal that surrounded the acclamation of the novel arose, I imagine, more from the identity of the author than from the subject of her tale. Young unmarried ladies were not meant to speculate so closely on the moral dilemma of a heroine who fears to meet in an afterlife two men who have, with equal right and to her equal pleasure, possessed her physically. Amélie's social and literary reputation, at any rate, proved too lively for the Chanler and Astor families when John Armstrong Chanler wooed and won her in the same year which saw the triumph of *The Quick or the Dead?* They were skeptical about their dazzling Virginian in-law. Nothing that happened in the next few years was to dissipate their distrust.

The young Armstrong Chanlers, rich, beautiful, and a bit wild, went to London, which has always been a lionizing capital. Amélie was lionized. She was admired by society from Oscar Wilde to the Princess Louise. But her marriage deteriorated. Chanler was bitterly jealous of her success. He came of a family of strong-willed egoists, more brilliant than creative, who, while quick to mock the trappings of courts, were never too proud to play jesters — provided that everybody looked at them. In her best novel, *Shadows of Flames*, Amélie described the plight of a beautiful poetess who makes two disastrous

136

marriages, to a dope addict and to an alcoholic. She told me that Chanler used to sleep with a revolver under his pillow, threatening that one night he would do what Archduke Rudolf had done at Mayerling. Finally, she divorced him.

At some point in her life she took to morphine — I suppose it was then. She assured me that she soon broke the habit and never went back to it. How she did it, I do not know, but the first part of *Shadows of Flames*, where Cecil Chesney and his wife battle with the drug, must have been inspired by a shattering personal experience. She related to me how once at the opera in New York, while her hand was resting on the velvet-covered partition between the boxes, it was clasped by a woman's hand, and she heard a voice murmur: "Don't look around, but tell me, oh, please tell me, how you did it!" Amélie whispered of her struggles while staring down at the fingers on which, in the dim light, she could make out immense jewels. When she had finished, the hand disappeared, and she heard the rustle of a dress. The lights went up for the entr'acte, and the neighboring box was empty. But she knew that it belonged to one of the richest families in New York. Amélie's stories were always like this: halfway between a startling truth and a tale in *True Romances*, but mellowed with time and nostalgia.

She was introduced to Pierre Troubetzkoy, whom she married in 1896, by Oscar Wilde. The marriage was an immensely happy one and lasted for forty years. Troubetzkoy, whose father had been banished from the Russian court for marrying an opera singer, made a moderate living as a fashionable portrait painter. Amélie took up writing fiction, poetry, and drama on a serious and regular basis. Once they tried an experiment. He would write a novel, and she would paint a portrait. The result of this compact was a sorry tale called *The Passer By* which was published by Doubleday with Amélie's amateur portrait of the heroine as a frontispiece. But domestically it was a mark of their happy communion.

I suppose they must have spent what they both earned (the combination of Russian aristocrat and a Virginia poetess hardly suggests economy), for in their later years they lived entirely at Castle Hill, and after Pierre's death, Amélie had little income. Somehow things were kept going. There was an arrangement with two former servants, who were allowed to farm the land in return for cooking and cleaning. Checks came in occasionally from old New York friends. Even the newspaper was a Christmas present. Repairs were dispensed with. But this near indigence was optional. At all times Castle Hill could have been sold for a sum that would have maintained Amélie and her sister in affluence in their few remaining years.

"But where would I live?" she used to wail to me, like Madame Ranevsky in *The Cherry Orchard*. "In some horrid, vulgar little apartment in Charlottesville? What would be the point of that? I should never be able to breathe away from Castle Hill. It is the only life I have left."

Castle Hill remained hers till her death.

*   *   *

I used to drive out to Castle Hill of a Saturday afternoon, sometimes alone, sometimes taking friends. After the brief gloom of my law school start I was happy in Charlottesville. Jefferson's university was too civilized a place to foster the neurotic form of puritanism that I had tried to bring to it. The law and the white columns of the Lawn and the beautiful countryside of red earth and blue hills blended in my imagination to create a vision of a life where more things were compatible than I had dreamed of. And Castle Hill was there to offer a balance to torts and contracts, to writs and cases — a glimpse into a past of almost inconceivable romance.

Amélie did most of the talking, but this was because I wanted it so. She talked with charm and wit and wisdom about her Virginia childhood, her life in London, in New York, in

Rome, her books and plays, the extraordinary people she had known. She would mimic the long dead with wonderful facial contortions, and her constant, high-pitched laughter seemed to clear away all the ghosts of pretension. She described the naiveté and pomposity of New York society in the nineties, the long, dull, sumptuous dinners and the childish self-importance of the hostesses. She made that life as vivid as the Charles Dana Gibson cartoons of it, and indeed it was easy to visualize her in the center of one of the latter, a Gibson girl, sitting, beautiful but detached, in a gilded salon with a balloon over her head showing the Virginia plantation of which she was dreaming.

Of course, I read all her novels. They were heady stuff, super-romantic, at times even "slushy." She was remarkably objective in discussing them and had few illusions about being a major novelist. Her wisdom had come, I sensed, late in life, possibly with the steadying influence of Pierre Troubetzkoy. A great charm in her fiction was the constant note of her love of Virginia. As in each of Trollope's novels there has to be a hunting chapter in deference to the author's greatest passion, so in Amélie Rives's the heroine must be Virginia born and must make at least one trip home in the course of her story. I should go so far as to say that Amélie's central theme was nostalgia for her native state and for Castle Hill. When she returned at last to live there permanently she wrote fewer books, probably because her emotional need was less. She was a kind of Emily Brontë in valentine.

Her heroines are terrible choosers of men, but their bad choices take them to splendid places: to great English houses, to ancient Italian palazzi, to Newport villas, to Fifth Avenue mansions. Passion crackles about their every step, and they are forever confusing it with love. Yet for all their agonizing, for all their yielding, they remain oddly unspoiled. The fates of Emma Bovary and Anna Karenina are not for them. The bright innocence of a Virginia childhood could apparently survive a good deal of tarnish. At the end one could always come home to Castle Hill.

The people and episodes of the stories are drawn directly from Amélie's life. Oscar Wilde makes a brief appearance in *Shadows of Flames* as Oswald Tyne, and in a dinner conversation with Sophie, the heroine, he exposes his deepest grievance with society:

"It is that no one will believe in my real wickedness — my beautiful vileness. I have no disciple who really believes in me. . . . But Sin, with the clear black flames curled about her naked feet like the petals of a lotus — Sin with her delicate, acrid lips that never satiate and are never satiated — her I worship? Her I serve! Do you believe me?"

Sophie is about to answer him in the same mocking vein when she is seized with a sudden conviction that he is speaking only the truth. She looks him straight in the eye and cries, "Yes!" The incident has no further consequences in the novel. If Amélie thought she was describing an actual incident, she may have been using a bit of hindsight. She knew Wilde before his trial; she wrote *Shadows of Flames* after it. Yet there is no doubt that she believed that she had intuitions and divinations beyond the scope of other mortals.

*   *   *

My feeling that the Amélie I knew was a larger and more generous woman than the author of *The Quick or the Dead?* was confirmed by her one-time sister-in-law, Mrs. Winthrop Chanler. The latter, who had called on her at Castle Hill in 1888, shortly before her engagement to John Armstrong Chanler, describes the meeting in *Roman Spring*:

"The beautiful Amélie did not appear for some time; when she finally did the effect was dazzling, especially to the young men. She had the largest dark blue-gray eyes; the longest black lashes; the most wonderful halo of loosely curled ash-blonde hair; very regular features, and a shapely, well-curved mouth. A romantic white tea gown draped and flowed from her shoulders in most becoming fashion, all but concealing her want of stature. She was full of life and had a slight Southern drawl that was attractive. A siren, a goddess, perhaps a genius — at all events we were well repaid for our expedition."

Mrs. Chanler goes on to report that for all Amélie's gifts, she lacked discipline, that her work suffered from an absence of technique. Her letters, which in the nineties had struck Mrs. Chanler as inspired, seemed, when looked over decades later, mere "shriveled flowers." Yet when she revisited Castle Hill, some forty years after her first visit, she was surprised and gratified to find that the "dangerous goddess," as she had once termed Amélie, had turned into a wise and charming old lady. I was put in mind of Talleyrand's statement: "After eighty, there are no enemies — only survivors."

I think my greatest regret when I finally began not only to write but publish novels was that I could not show them to Amélie. She had asked to see my work, but, rather churlishly, I would never give it to her. While I was at law school I had locked it all away. But she was always emphatic that I should not give it up. Recently, while I was turning over some old notes and papers, I came upon a letter that Amélie had written me in 1938 to describe a conversation which she had had with one of my professors at the Law School. She had written:

"I saw my dear friend Leslie Buckler about two weeks ago, and he stayed with me nearly three hours. We talked of you, and he said some things that will show you how keenly observant he is though he does not seem so.

"I asked him how he thought you were getting on with the study of law, and this is what he replied:

" 'Very well indeed — excellently. But there's something. I find him an unusual boy. Keen and sensitive in the best meaning of that word. But the something I mentioned is this. I feel that his will and brain are concentrated on his study of law, but — his whole *heart* isn't in it.'

"I didn't say anything for a few seconds, then I asked:

" 'Do you think that will interfere with his coming out on top?'

" 'No,' said Leslie. 'He will come out all right. It's only that one's heart must be in it — to devote one's whole life to the law.'

"Then (I hope you'll forgive me, dear Louis, but we were talking confidentially and I thought at least there shouldn't be any mystery about it) then I said:

" 'The truth is, Leslie, that the chief thing in his heart is to be a writer. *I* think, though he has never even hinted anything of the kind to me, that he is devoted to his father, and is studying law to please him. I know, when I asked to see some of his manuscripts he replied that he had locked them all away in New York when he decided to come to the University of Virginia and study law. So you see, though his heart mayn't be in it his will and mind and determination *are* in it.'

" 'Good,' said Leslie. 'He will come out.' "

AILEEN TONE
AND HENRY ADAMS

BECAUSE I MARRIED LATE and lived as a bachelor only a few blocks from my parents' apartment, many of their friends, who had been rather remote figures in my childhood, became friends of mine as well. One of these was Aileen Tone. She was a very beautiful old maid, older than my parents, with an exquisite charm of manner, a silver voice, and an unerring eye for the first rate in art and poetry. She never seemed quite to belong to our century, yet she was perfectly at home in it. George Meredith might have described her as a realist in porcelain.

Her name had always been bracketed in my mind with that of Henry Adams, whose books I vastly admired. She had been his "secretary-companion and adopted niece" and had presided over his household in Lafayette Square, directly across from the White House. Her job, as he had put it, was "to keep him alive," and she had succeeded for five years, until the winter of 1918.

Aileen survived "Uncle Henry" by more than half a century. In her little apartment on East 83rd Street in Manhattan, before the mantel over which hung the drawing of Adams by

John Briggs Potter (until it was taken away by the Adams family to Quincy and placed in a dark room to prevent it from fading), she kept his image fresh. I remember, after the bombing of Hiroshima, her quoting from his poem to the Virgin of Chartres: "Seize, then, the Atom! rack his joints!" Scholars and biographers of Adams and of Adams's friends — Harold Dean Cater, Ernest Samuels, Leon Edel, Edward Chalfant — came to listen and to hear the past made vivid.

For years, I was a regular monthly caller at Aileen's, stopping in at six after work. She read my books and made shrewd and helpful comments on them. She guided my reading, particularly in French literature. She was always a special presence, a reminder that one did not have to live exclusively in the world of immediate experience. This was not, either, because she turned away from life in the rough; her tolerant Catholicism kept her from that error. She simply pleaded for equal time for the exquisite, knowing that it did not take power or money to achieve it, but only a little patience, a little industry. Aileen was a kind of lay priestess, with a wise, worldly side to her kindness and understanding. She put me in mind of an eighteenth-century French abbess, who knew that life had to be kept constantly fresh, constantly vivid, that one must never neglect one's mind or one's heart or one's clothes or one's accent. She stood for style in the deepest sense of that word.

Of course we often talked about Adams, but in the last two years of her life we began to do so more intently. To me *The Education of Henry Adams* and *Mont-Saint-Michel and Chartres* have always represented a summit in American prose. I can think of no other books where the sentences are so hard and clear and yet so deeply embedded with emotion. I was curious about the man in old age as revealed to Aileen, and she was increasingly disposed to talk about him. I suppose as her own end approached she realized that her years with Adams had been the great chapter of her life, and I think that she wanted, and at the same time did not want, some memorial of them.

Gradually I began to piece together the story of how Adams and Aileen had met and become friends. Childless and a widower, he had become dependent on his own and his wife's nieces. The avuncular role appealed to him, both as man and writer. Nephews, he maintained, "as a social class" had given up reading, which ruled them out for the scholar, but nieces were different. The relationship between uncle and niece was "convenient and easy, capable of being anything or nothing, at the will of either party, like a Mohammedan or Polynesian or American marriage." He wrote *Mont-Saint-Michel and Chartres* as a series of talks by an uncle to a niece, either an actual niece or one who was willing to be a niece in wish. Aileen, as a niece in wish, was to bring to perfection a relationship that had begun as an only half-serious idea.

She met him through Mrs. Bancel LaFarge and Mrs. Ward Thoron, nieces of Mrs. Adams. As a member of the Schola Cantorum, Aileen had learned piano arrangements for old French songs, which she sang to Adams, who was fascinated. He found in their atonalities a possibility of recapturing the music of the twelfth-century poems that he so loved. He delighted in their unexpected conclusions. "They end with their tails in the air," he used to say. The friendship deepened. Adams became disturbed when Aileen was away. "Come back, poor wanderer!" he wrote her in April of 1912, adding despondently: "But you won't." In September he wrote again:

"Truly come and bring me life in some form, for I perish. I am happy and content but cannot honestly grumble, which is a sort of suffocation. I cannot truthfully care even about Theodore [Roosevelt] and shall have four long years to admire Mr. Woodrow Wilson. The world has gone to the devil, and I smile with content. I, too, have gone to the devil. Come and entertain him."

145

Their need was mutual. He wanted a companion to look after him; Aileen had to support herself. It was agreed that she should become a permanent member of his household. At last he was able to say to her: "You must write your mother and tell her you are never coming home." But, of course, she still had to visit Mrs. Tone in New York, and Adams was much fretted during these necessary absences. The following are excerpts from a series of notes he sent up from Washington:

"I have nothing to say, except that as soon as your mother is tired of you, I wish you would remember the next train. Like Richard [the Lion-Hearted], I make no reproaches, *mais pourtant je suis seul. Comtesse Soeur* [Richard's form of address to his sister], may you make all your family happy — don't neglect anyone — but by and by sing a Pastourelle for the poor Robin [shepherd in a *chante-fable*]. . . . Of course without you I am quite helpless, and count the hours till you return. . . . Everything has stopped running since you went away. . . . Apparently Mrs. Jones' orders that I must not be disturbed are likely to end in my burial without clergy. *Tant mieux.* I don't really care. . . . Your letters are my only excitement. . . . Florence has gone to Florida. Her father is said to be dying. So am I! A lunch yesterday did it. You had better come soon if you want to see me first."

The relationship between the old widower, an impatient perfectionist intolerant of the least sloppiness in thought or manners, and the beautiful, much-alive younger woman was at first not easy, but the devotion and understanding that existed between them triumphed in the end. Adams to Aileen was always the great man, with the wisdom and knowledge of the noblest philosopher, and she to him represented the beauty and grace, the feminine subtlety and sympathy, that he found indispensable to a civilized life. This Platonic union was to be closer than most marriages.

Adams in his old age occupied a unique position in Washington. Sought out by the many, he held himself aloof, limiting his company to those who would amuse him or to those (even fewer) who could give him insight in his incessant and ultimately obsessive quest for a scientific formula that would explain the history of man. Not all admired him. To some he was moody and misanthropic; a rich, spoiled man who had to have his way in everything or else he sulked, a frustrated statesman who despised the world because he had not achieved its temporal as well as its intellectual honors. But to his family and intimates he was a cult, to American historians he was a master, and to subsequent generations he has become a seer whose dark vision of our century has been terribly justified. If Adams, as Justice Holmes said, liked to play the role of the wise and cynical old cardinal, sitting alone by the fire and enjoying the fact that the world came to him without his going to the world, his cynicism has more to say to us today than Holmes's speeches on the need for war to keep a nation virile.

I noted, as Aileen and I talked, that her thoughts kept turning back to the summer of 1914. She had been with Adams and his niece Elsie in France at the outbreak of war. He had rented the Château de Coubertin just north of Paris, and there they were stuck without automobiles or horses until such time as they could arrange transportation home. Adams finally got hold of a horse that had not yet been fully broken and had it hitched to a carriage for the afternoon drive. His driver had been told by its owner that the creature must not be whipped, yet the first thing the idiot did was to strike it, and the little party was carried away at a gallop across country while Adams hooted with laughter. Somehow, as Aileen described that laughter, I had the feeling that it was the only laughter in France, the desperate, frustrated laughter of an old man who had survived to the Armageddon that he had predicted.

One day they explored a medieval tower in the neighborhood, and Aileen climbed to the top to see the view. Police arrived and booked the party of three as possible spies. At the station Adams became so indignant at the questions of the magistrate that he could no longer remember anything. Asked for his grandmother's name, he turned to Aileen and shouted: "What the devil was my grandmother's name?"

They finally went to Dieppe and thence to England, where they occupied Sir Ronald Lindsay's house in Stepleton in Dorset, walking in the countryside and haunted by the sense of distant battle. Henry James came down from London to spend the night, and he and Adams sat up late talking. Aileen, as she thought tactfully, absented herself, but the next morning Adams told her that she should have stayed. He made it very clear that she was never to leave him. The beautiful English fall, the peaceful fields and woods, the old, distinguished, talking men, the death of youth across the Channel — it was the leavetaking of two eras.

It was after Aileen had told me of this final meeting between the two great Henrys that I conceived of a formal plan to catch and preserve her reminiscences. I proposed that she relate to me, in a more or less chronological fashion, at weekly sessions, the story of her life with Adams. It would not be a "ghost" arrangement. I should be a dictaphone, pure and simple. I knew that it would be hopeless to get Aileen to utter a word if I took so much as a note in her presence or used a machine. My only chance would be to chat with her about Adams, gradually reducing my role in the conversation as her interest quickened. After each talk I would go straight home and write down what I remembered while it was still fresh in my mind. Very hesitantly, she agreed to give it a try.

I had learned my method in 1943 in navy courts-martial in the Panama Canal Zone when I was appointed to represent some poor sailor who was obviously guilty. The only hope of diminishing his inevitable sentence was to offer to the court what was called a "statement in mitigation." This had to be delivered by the defendant himself, and if it had obviously been written by the lawyer, it did not have much effect on the court. I therefore adopted the practice of spending a good deal of time alone with the defendant, writing and rewriting his penitent confession until I had it in exactly his words. I would then make him recite it to me while I coached him in ways to make it sound sincere. He was the actor, I the director. (I had a fair degree of success with my method but it ultimately got me in trouble. In my last court-martial the presiding officer congratulated the defendant on his "frank and honest" statement and gave him the minimum penalty. But he then proceeded to censure me as a lazy, good-for-nothing counsel who had done nothing but plead guilty and leave the job of defense to my poor client. What could I say? I could hardly explain that the "frank and honest" statement had been a work of art!)

After each meeting with Aileen I inscribed my impression of what she had said. But when, after the second, I showed her my transcript, she was much distressed. "Because it is so wrong?" I asked. "No, because it is so right," she said sadly, "and I'm so wrong." She could not go on with our sessions. I know that what disturbed her was the impression that she feared she might have given of remembering too keenly the initial difficulties of her position in Adams's household. Obviously, it had not been easy for a beautiful younger woman to enter the home of an ailing old man, adored by a jealous family, and adapt herself to the rigorous routine that he had long established. As will be seen, there were moments of loneliness and frustration. But to me these fragments show how both the uncle and the adopted niece turned their relationship into something extraordinarily beautiful.

Aileen knew that I would try to put these fragments into a piece about her and Adams after her death, and I believe she did not mind. She simply did not want anything of that nature

149

to appear in print during her lifetime. When she lay dying in July of 1969 at the age of ninety-one, and I went to say goodbye, she gave me the copy of the *Education* which Adams had given to her.

But now I shall let Aileen speak for herself. Here is a day in 1913:

"We always walked for an hour before breakfast, which we ate on trays in the living room by a fire. Then old Dawson, Uncle Henry's coachman, brought around the purple victoria that had once belonged to Perry Belmont, and we drove to Rock Creek Park. Uncle Henry knew its every path and turn, almost its every tree and bush, and he would plan a different walk for each morning, telling Dawson exactly where to meet us and just what time we would be there. We never failed to emerge from the park at the appointed hour and place.

"Lunch was at noon, and afterwards Uncle Henry would sleep until three. That was the hour for correspondence. I wrote out his letters in longhand under his dictation and then read him the financial news from the *New York Times*. He was particularly interested in the price of gold, which played so large a role in his and his brother Brooks's theories of history. On the dot of four Dawson would reappear with the victoria, and Uncle Henry would ask me if I had any errands or any calls to make. Sometimes, if I could think of none, we would simply sit in the stationary vehicle until he finally exclaimed, with a touch of impatience: 'All right, Dawson, to the river!'

"Oh, that river! I once protested to Uncle Henry that the air was so damp I thought we must be below sea level. 'But we *are* below sea level,' he replied.

"There were enormous compensations in life with a man of such wisdom and kindness and sympathy, but those afternoon drives were the bad part of my day. However, then came dinner, which Uncle Henry always made into a festive occasion.

We dressed, even when alone — he insisted that I should have good clothes and look well — and there was always champagne, which he would drink in such rapid gulps that I was sometimes afraid he would choke. 'It's the only way to taste good champagne,' he would retort if I protested.

"He never dined out, even when asked to the White House — 'I'm in bed with a nurse' was his invariable excuse — and he never asked people in, but he expected them to propose themselves. Young people were shy about this, but I soon learned to tell when he wanted company and would suggest to friends of my own, Robert and Mildred Bliss or Frank and Lily Polk, that they come in on a given night. In this way we had many pleasant parties. Uncle Henry was passionately curious to know what 'the young men were thinking,' but he could never bear to feel that they had come out of obligation to an old man. The impulse for the meeting had to be all on their part."

Aileen believed that one of Adams's great disappointments was that he did not appeal more to young men. He would have adored to have been surrounded by a crowd of disciples as was Justice Holmes, of whom in this respect he was very jealous. Judge Learned Hand told me once how vividly he remembered Adams's snort and his "Very interesting, very interesting" when Hand told him that Holmes was the man he admired most in the world. Adams's interest in young men, however, diminished if they had not come to the house to talk to *him*. Aileen did not have an easy time when her own friends came.

"I remember one awkward afternoon when a friend of mine from the British embassy called on me, and Uncle Henry refused to leave the room and was so icy that the poor young man never came again. Also, he hated to have me go out without him; if I cared about a party, I had to beg permission to attend. He would cross-examine me about my prospective host and hostess and why I wanted to go, and he could be very disparaging indeed when he wanted to be. But in the end he would always yield and say with a sigh: 'It seems I must send you forth, a dove from my ark.' The next morning, of course, he would want to know every detail about the party, who was there and what was said. He was quick to discover just how little he had missed."

Then there came the terrible day, the day on which the whole plan of their life threatened to crumble.

"One evening when some old but not very interesting acquaintances of Uncle Henry's had proposed themselves for dinner, the conversation was going very slowly. He was obviously bored, and rather thunderously silent, and I tried, in my nervousness, to save the party with small talk. The next morning in the victoria Uncle Henry said gruffly and suddenly: 'My dear, you were a bore last night.'

"I shall never forget the pain of that moment! To be called a bore, of all things! By Uncle Henry, who could never suffer bores! I was almost blinded by the soreness of it; I was like some desperate hurt creature; I even tried to get out of the carriage. Then Uncle Henry grabbed my wrist and said, very clearly and firmly: 'Listen to me, and I will tell you why you were a bore, and then you need never be one again. You were a bore last night because you talked about yourself. There! It's as simple as that! And now we shan't have to worry about it in the future.' "

Aileen was not possessed of independent means, and it had been understood from the beginning that she should receive a salary. She was always perfectly sensible and practical about such matters, but to Adams these considerations seemed to place a blot on their high friendship.

"My first monthly paycheck was agony to him. He had a habit of keeping money in drawers all over the house, and on the day when my check was due he called me into his study and abruptly pulled open a drawer full of bills. 'Take it!' he exclaimed in the tone of one performing an impossibly distasteful duty. 'Take it all, I beg of you!' I insisted on taking only what was my due and proceeded to count out the correct amount. 'This is impossible,' he cried, and the next week he summoned his nephew Charles Adams from Boston to draw up a deed of trust. By the terms of this trust he gave me an income for my life, regardless of whether or not I should remain in his household. 'Now you are independent,' he told me with satisfaction. 'You can leave me tomorrow if you choose.' But if he offered me a world of liberty with one hand, I was glad that with the other he held me to his side. This may sound possessive on his part, and perhaps it was, but Uncle Henry was old and lonely, and I had come to him of my own free will. He was terribly conscious of the sacrifice that I might be making in choosing the life that I had chosen. 'When I first suggested that you stay,' he told me ruefully, 'I thought I had only a few months to live. And now, look what has happened. I go on and on.' "

Mrs. Adams had committed suicide in 1885, almost thirty years before Aileen joined Adams's household, but her memory was always present in the very absence of references to her. All Adams's family maintained a virtual conspiracy of silence on the theory that the subject was agonizing to Adams, that even a passing reference would cause him pain. Yet he and Aileen very frequently visited the tomb in Rock Creek Cemetery with the beautiful brooding statue by Saint-Gaudens. She felt that the silence was artificial, and at last she broke it.

"I said to him in the carriage: 'Uncle Henry, I cannot bear that we never mention Aunt Clover. Won't you tell me about her?' He said: 'My dear child, I should like nothing better.' We went back to the house, and he spent hours showing me photographs of his wife and pictures of things that they had seen together. When I asked him why he had never spoken of her, he said that he had been made to feel that any reference to her would be painful to his family."

In the last, long winter of Adams's life Aileen, constantly on duty, almost wore herself out.

"I was so tired that winter. I have never before or since been so tired. Elsie Adams used to say to me, 'Vous faites pitié.' She urged me to go away, but I knew that I could not, and I knew that Uncle Henry could not spare me. I can only hope that he did not know how tired I was. I tried so hard to conceal it. No, I do not think that he ever knew.

"But at last I did go away — just for a weekend. I had been asked to stay with Mr. and Mrs. Nelson Fell in Virginia. It was a small house party, and Mrs. Fell made such a point of my coming that I agreed to go. I worried about Uncle Henry every minute. Finally I became so nervous that I called the house in Washington. Elsie Adams answered the telephone and tried to reassure me about Uncle Henry. I told her I was coming straight home. She insisted that it was not necessary, but I came anyway. When I got to the house I hurried upstairs, where I found Uncle Henry sitting with Elizabeth Hoyt, who was reading aloud to him. I went straight over to his side and knelt down by the low chair and put my arms around him. He was a little man, you know, and I could feel his whole body trembling. 'Never leave me, never leave me,' he murmured, and I replied, 'I never will.' Two days later, when I went into his room in the morning, I found him dead."

Index

INDEX

157

INDEX

159

A WRITER'S CAPITAL